Olga Shmatova

# Techniques
# Gouache Painting
# for Beginners

## vol. 1

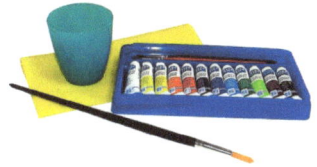

2010

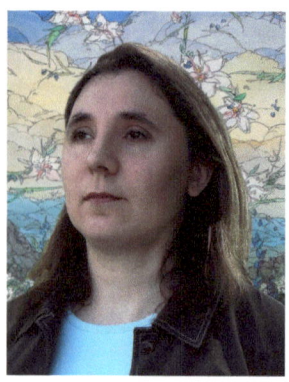

# Techniques Gouache Painting for Beginners vol.1

## Olga Shmatova

## Gouache

Gouache colors are popular with many designers, but they can used also for painting.

Rich choice of colors and easy mixing, quick drying and easy correcting, odorless and does not require bulky equipment. All this are made gouache an excellent choice for beginner painter. Work in gouache can be easily switch to other paint: oil or acrylic.

Olga Shmatova

**The author thanks for providing pictures of his students:**

Christina Krey
Irina Guseva
Naila Alyautdinova
Elena Stepanova
Elena Petracheva
Tatiana Korotkih
Marina Kurdyukova
Alexey Petrov

idea, text, schemes, illustrations and design by Olga Shmatova

photos by Sergey Kuzmichev
translate by Sergey Kuzmichev

This is third publication (fully modification) 2010 year
First publication 2005 year by EKSMO, Moskow

error

picture by beginner painter

**http://artolbook.com**

# Table of Content

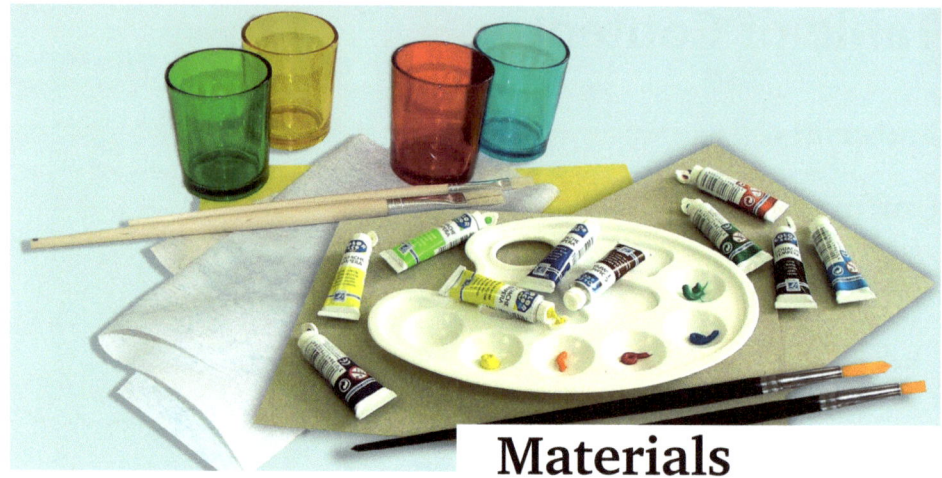

# Materials

For employment are needed:

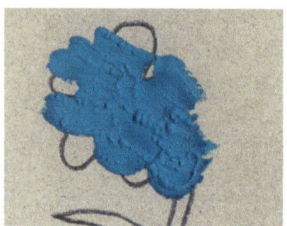

Very liquid paint.

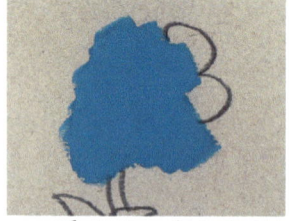

Very thick paint.

The paint is normal consistency.

Sheet of paperboard is attached to tablet with paper tape.

# Paint
Gouache set of 12 colors.

# Brushes
Syntetic round brush No 7
Syntetic flat brush No 4

# Support
A few sheets of paperboard 20x30 sm (8x12 in), 200 g/m2 (53 lb) or thicker. Sheet will

# For drawing
Pencil 3b and eraser

# Tablet
The tablet is used as hard support for sheets. Tablets are made of plywood or hardboard. The area of your tablet should be larger then the area of sheet.

# Paper adhesive tape
Sheets is attached to the tablet with paper adhesive tape.

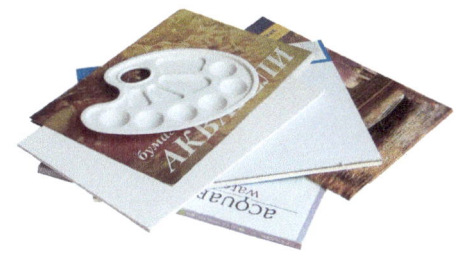

The plastic palette.

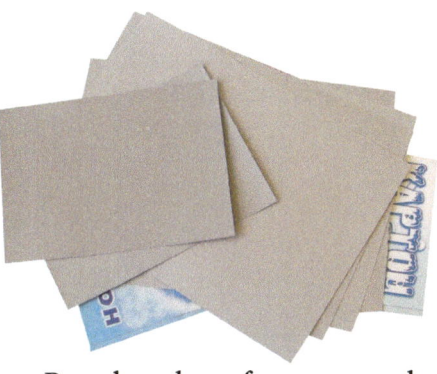

Paperboard for gouache painting.

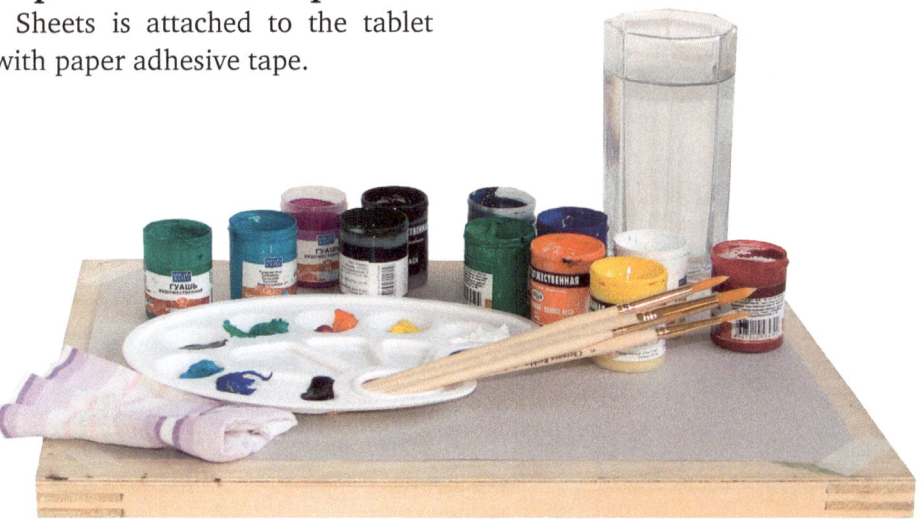

Painting equipment.

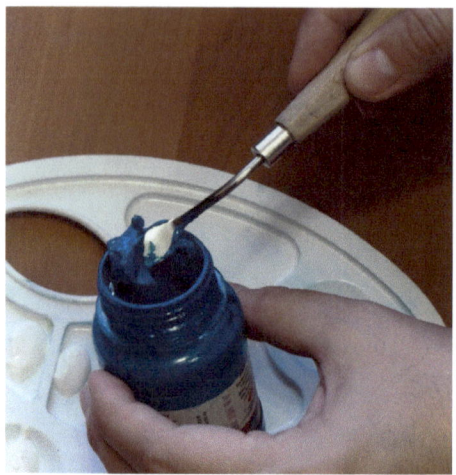

The paint is convenient taking out from jar with painting knife.

The jars of paint should be open in work time.

## Palette

The palette is used for paint and color mixing. For gouache is used plastic palettes. The palette should be white. In an extreme case it may be replaced disposable plate. More convenient to use two or three palettes.

## Jar of water

Water is used for washing brushes and dilution paint. Jar should be no less 200 ml (6 oz).

## Rag for brushes

Brushes are wiped with a rag. If do otherwise, then water will be transfered on palette with brush. Over time paint on palette will be very liquid.

## Painting knife

Painting knife is used to move a paint on the palette from jar. If your used paint tubes, then painting knife not needed.

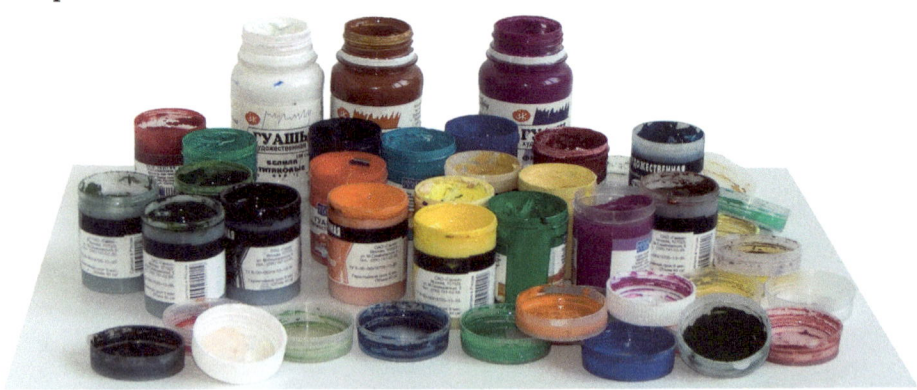

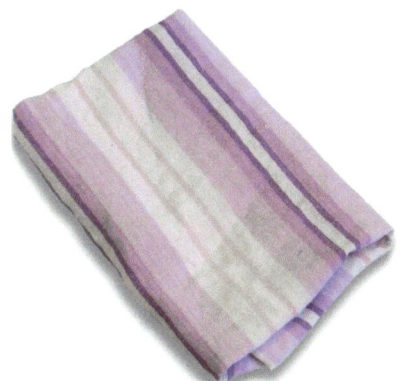

The rag for wiping brushes.

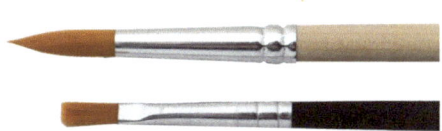

The syntetic round brush No 7 and syntetic flat brush No 4.

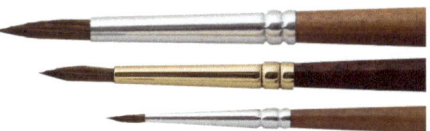

The sable brush can used for gouache painting.

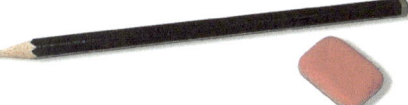

The simple pencil and eraser.

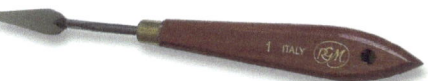

The painting knife.

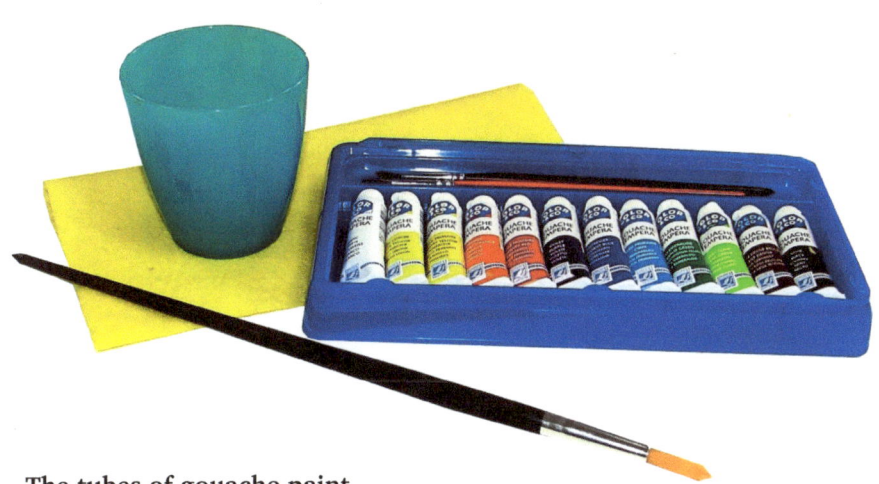

The tubes of gouache paint.

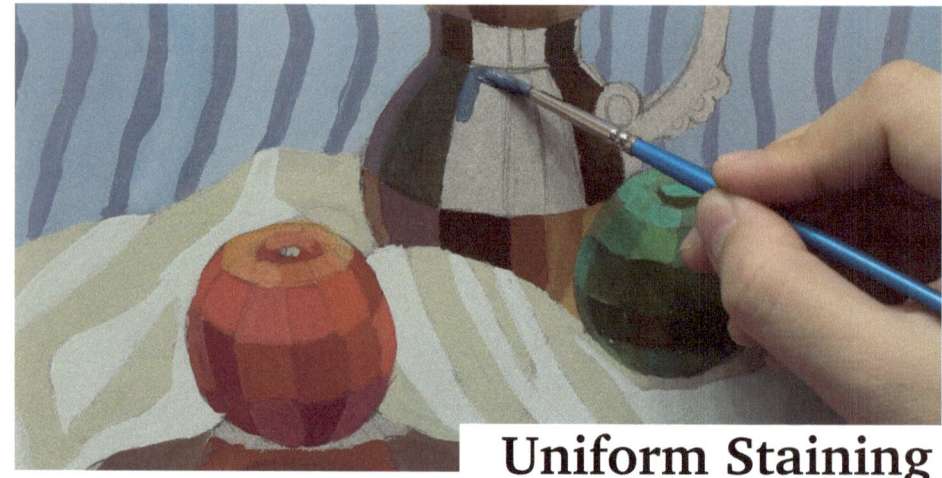

# Uniform Staining

Uniform staining this is to stain support with a thin and uniform paint layer.

Uniform staining is used to first paint layer. To apply paint the second and subsequent layers should with technique of opaque layers. The technique uniform staining most often uses as a basis for other techniques, such as softening edges.

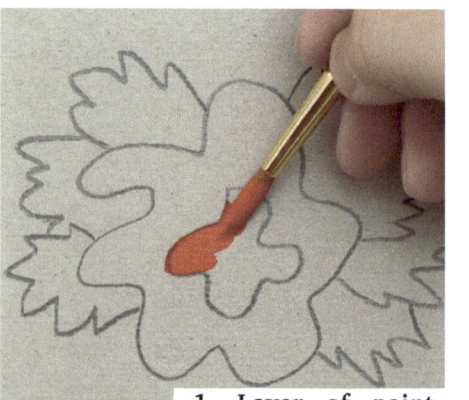

1. Layer of paint should be smooth without hillocks and spots. Therefore, the paint should be evenly distributed throughout the brush. Excess paint is removed on the edge of the palette. Start to stain from the edge of the spot.

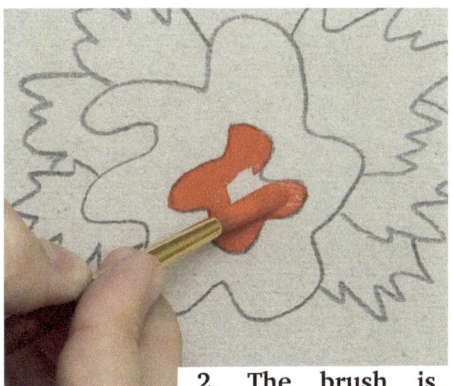

2. The brush is moved from edge to the center. Paint should be apply quickly, to it did not have time dry.

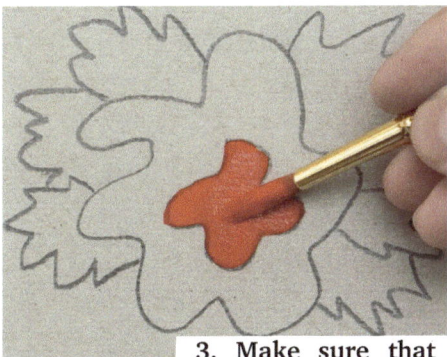

3. Make sure that on the surface not form puddles of excess paint. If a puddles of excess paint formed: excess paint is moved to the edge of staining area with brush. Then it is removed with a clean brush. The brush is cleaned with a rag.

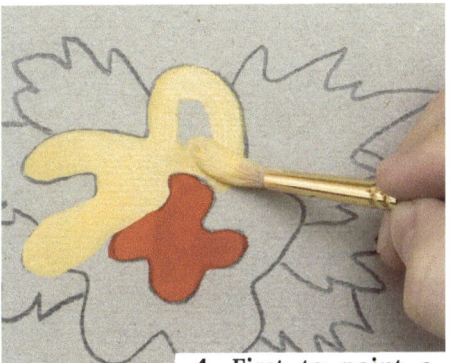

4. First to paint a edge. After that the area inside is painted.

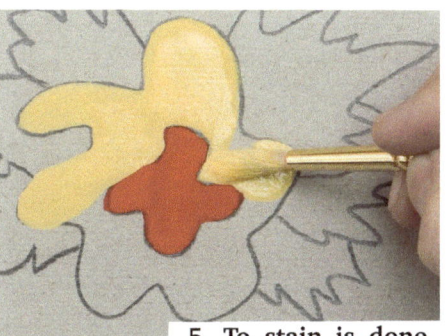

5. To stain is done in small areas and quickly.

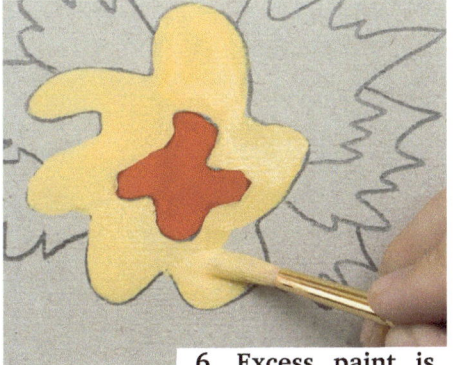

6. Excess paint is moved on unpainted area with a brush.

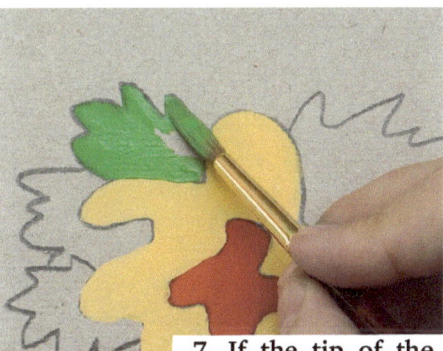

7. If the tip of the brush is not moved along the edge, the uniform stained area is got unlikely.

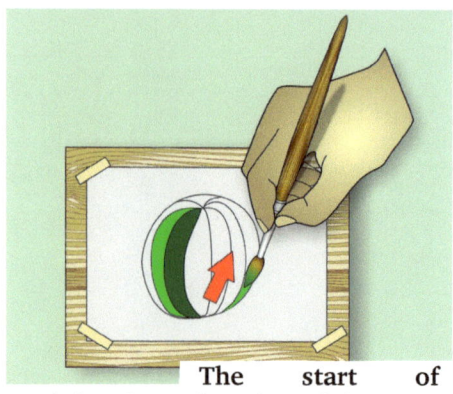

The start of staining from the edge of the spot. The brush should move parallel edge.

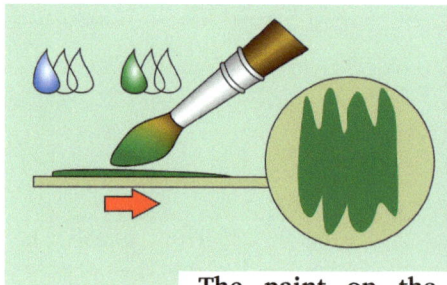

The paint on the brush should be a little and medium thickness.

## Stages of Technique

1. Gouache this a thick paint. So before you start painting, paint should be stirred to a state of uniform mass. Otherwise when the paint will dry its surface will be uneven. In addition: when a poorly mixed pigment and a binder of paint will dry, they will create light spots in dark halos.

The paint should be moderate thickness, but not be very liquid. Sufficiently consistency like liquid sour cream. Paint on the brush should be a little bit.

2. The brush should fit the shape area that will stained. For example: flat brush is convenient for staining rectangular parts of houses and windows.

3. Detail is stained from edge to the center. A paint should be wet on a sheet and a palette.

4. After stage three a detail is stained from center to the edge. Excess paint is moved to the edge of staining area with brush. Then it is removed with a clean brush. The brush is wiped with rag. Would a very good if a paint will be exactly as much as needed.

# Exercises

Take sheet 4x4 inch (10x10 cm). Draw with pencil on the sheet four squares. All sides of the square are equal. The first square with sides of 0,4 inch (1 cm), the second - with the sides 0,8 inch (2 cm), the third – 1,2 inch (3 cm), and the fourth – 1,6 inch (4 cm). Stain this squares smoothly without hillocks and spots. Remove excess paint with the brush. Remember: to uniform stain the small area use a small brush, for the large area use a large brush.

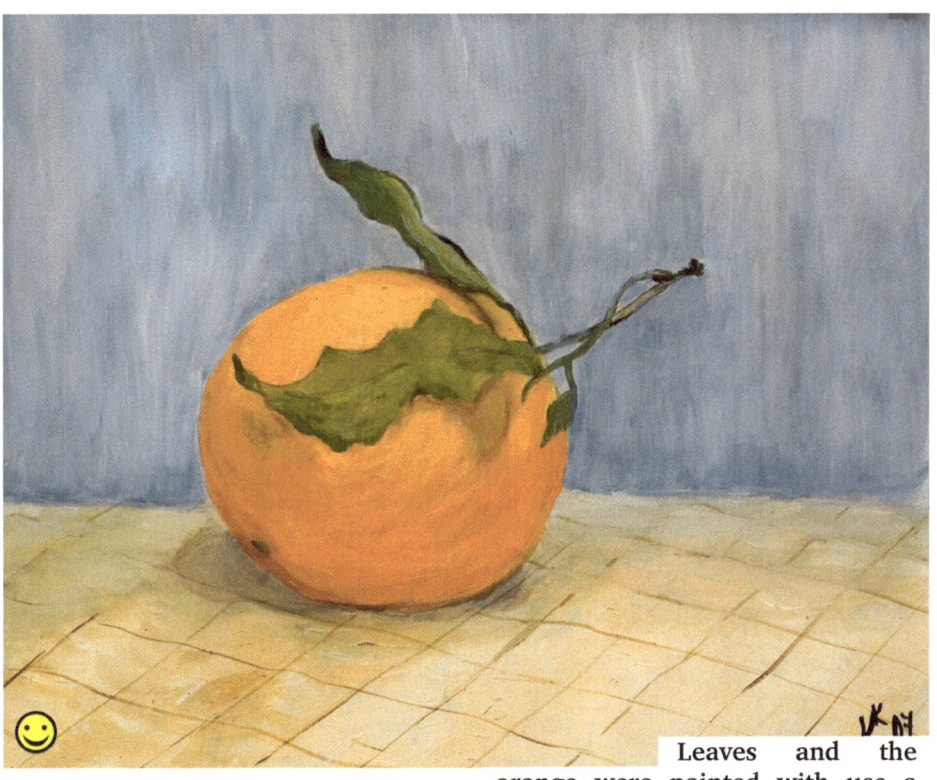

Leaves and the orange were painted with use a uniform staining. Layers of shadows and penumbra were applied thereafter.

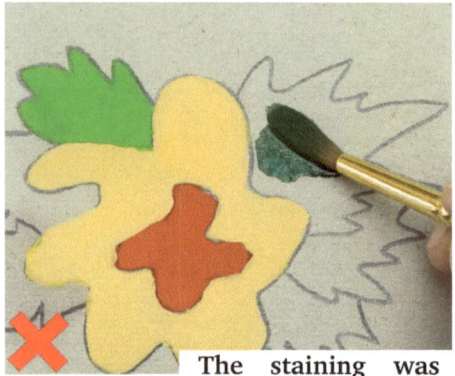

The staining was not started from edge.

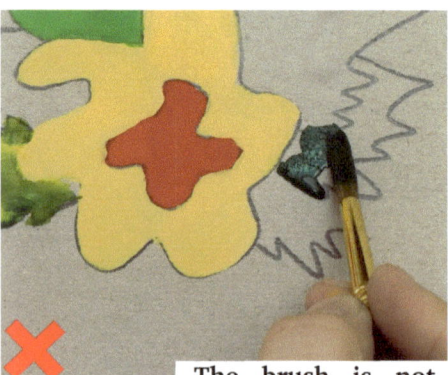

The paint of different shades on the brush.

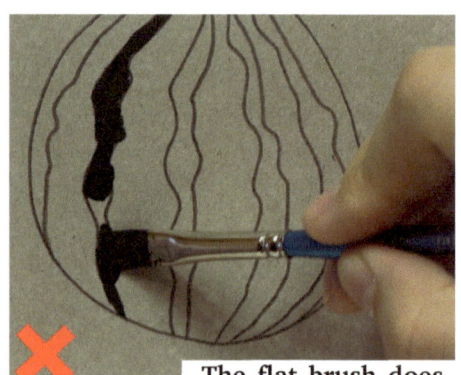

The flat brush does not fit for this area.

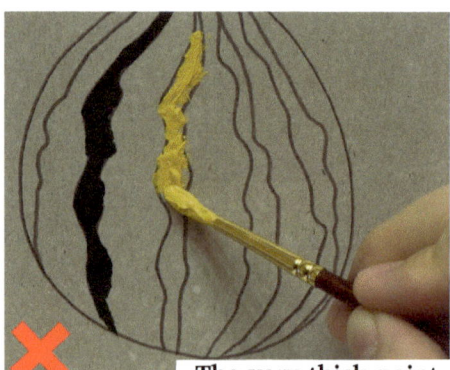

The very thick paint lays down uneven with lumps.

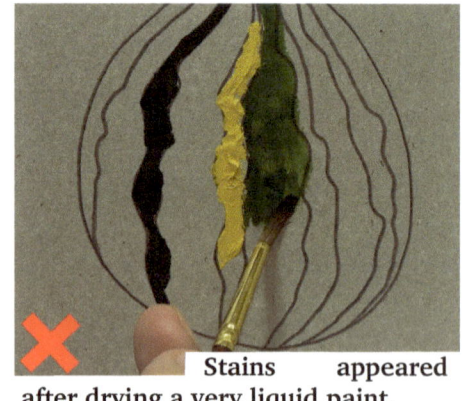

The brush is not moved along of edge. A lot of paint on the brush.

Stains appeared after drying a very liquid paint.

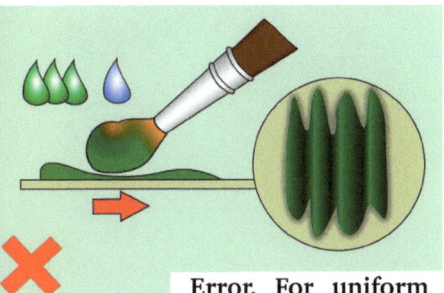

Error. For uniform staining a excess paint should not be on the brush.

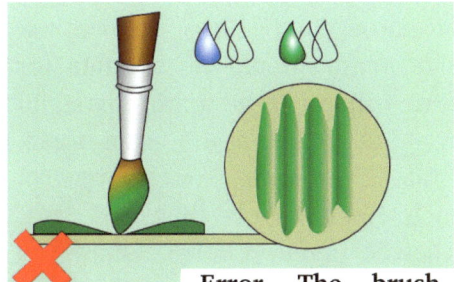

Error. The brush should be not vertically but at an angle to sheet.

## Most Frequent Errors

Very many paint on the brush.

The brush not fit to the shape of the stained area.

The paint too liquid or thick.

Staining is not parallel the edge.

The paint had dried because of too slow staining.

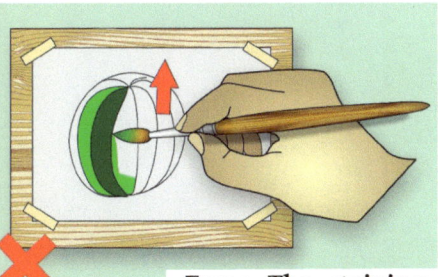

Error. The staining with entire plane of the brush.

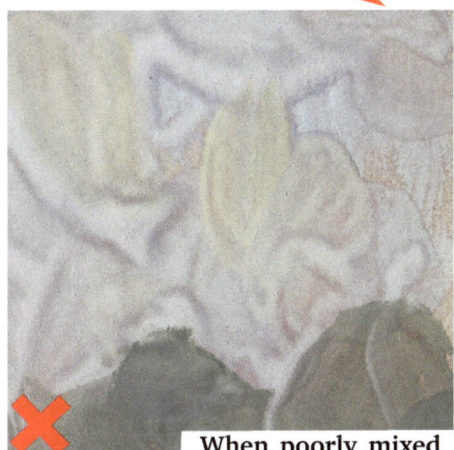

When poorly mixed pigment and a binder of paint will dry, they will create light spots in dark halos.

## Helpful Tips

Choose a brush with paying attention to the area of painting. The brush should be suitable for area which will be uniformly stain. For a large area use a large brush. Uniform staining area more 2x2 inch (5x5 cm) is thankless task. The technique uniform staining do not use for large area. For large area use the technique wash of uniform colors (wash without gradient).

Use a color mixture. Color mixtures lays down better than pure color (how is - from jar or tube).

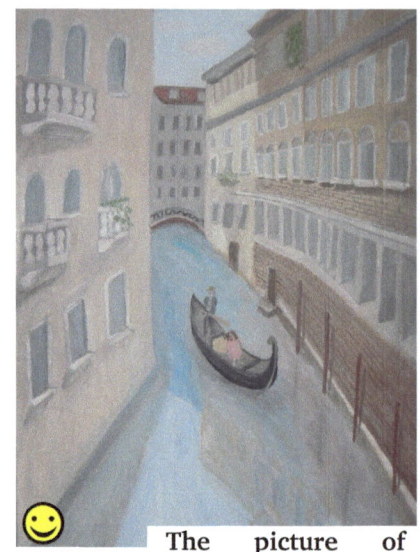

The picture of beginner painters was painted with use techniques: uniform staining, strokes and softening edges.

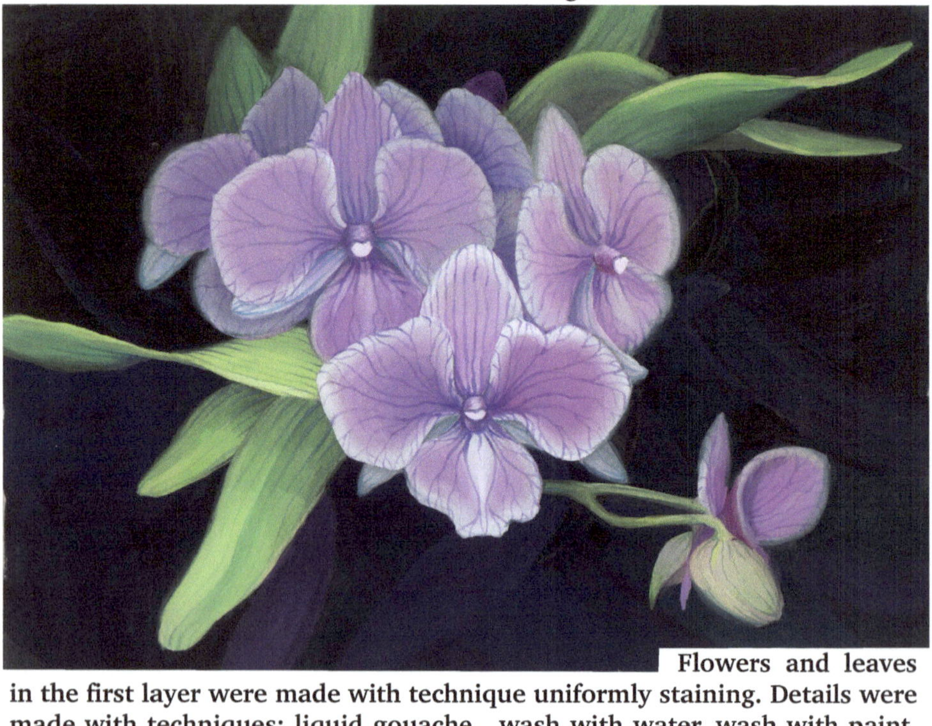

Flowers and leaves in the first layer were made with technique uniformly staining. Details were made with techniques: liquid gouache, wash with water, wash with paint, and softening edges.

# Compatibility with Other Techniques

Uniform staining can be used together with any techniques.

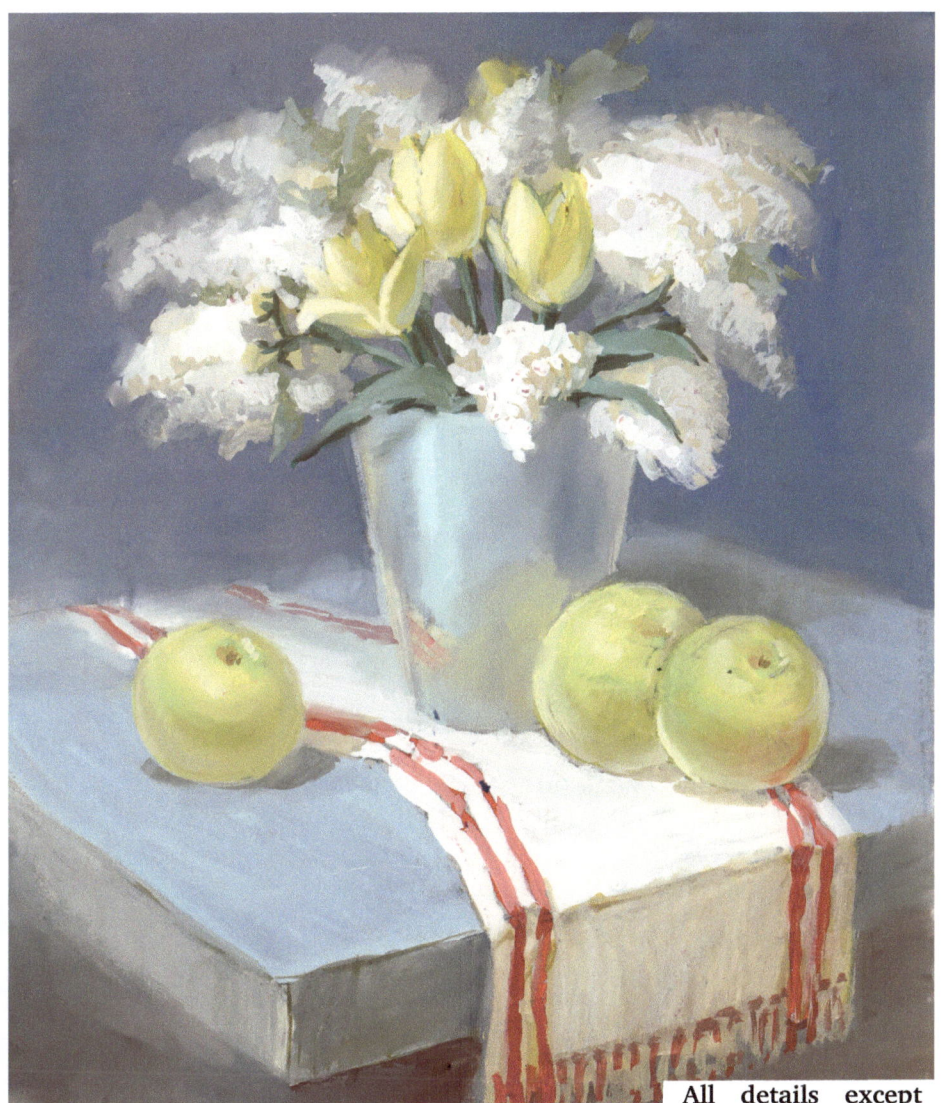

**All details except** background were made with uniform staining. After that was applied technique opaque layers. Dry layers are washed with water and paint. Little details were added with a liquid gouache.

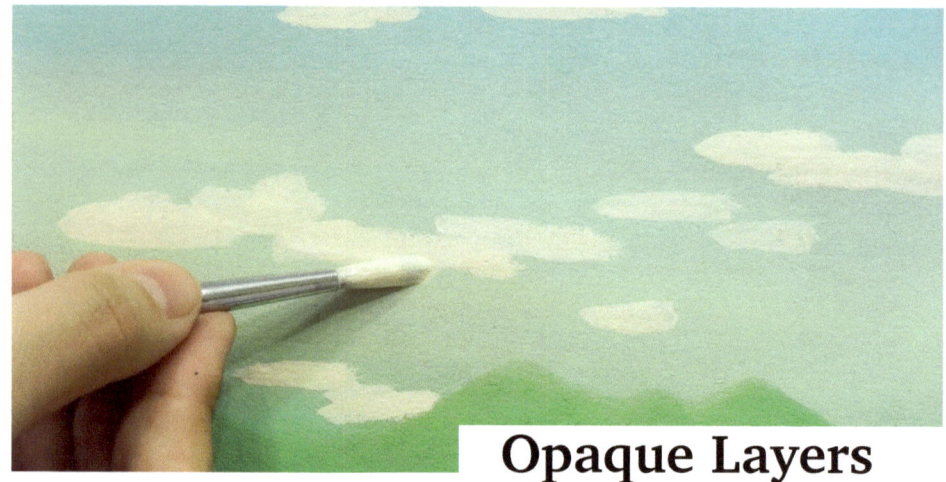

# Opaque Layers

**Popularity: 5 from 5**

Opaque layers use for to hide lower layers.

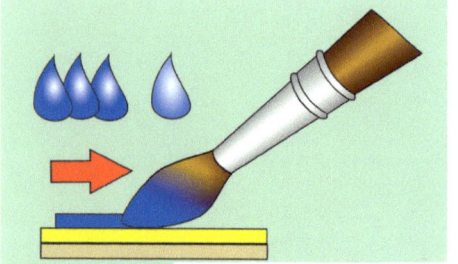

**The opaque layer is applied with brush with a lot of thick paint.**

During the creation picture often require overpaint to lower layer with a opaque paint. Dark colors on light background fit well, covering it without a stains, and gaps. Layers of light colors do not always completely cover the dark colors. This due to the properties of dark pigments of paints - they emerge through the layers. Overlaying with light colors on dark background can only with one (no more than two) quick stroke. Otherwise lower layer will be dissolved and blended with upper. This will wash with paint. Therefore a thick paint is applied only on a thoroughly dry background.

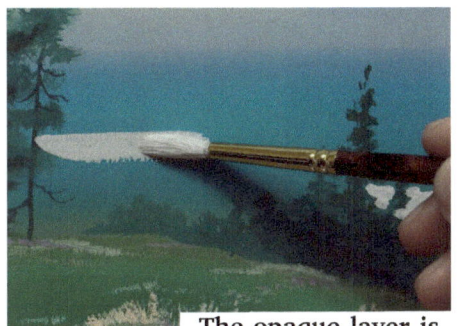

The opaque layer is applied rightly.

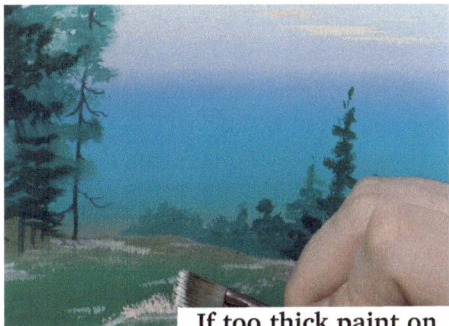

If too thick paint on the brush, then obtain the effect of dry brush.

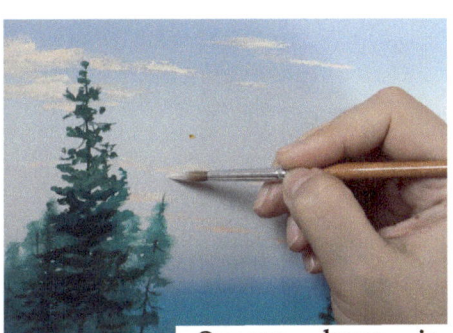

Opaque layer is applied with soft-hair brush, for example: sable.

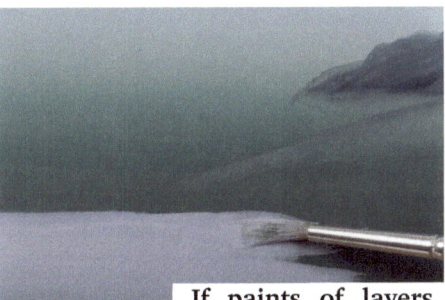

If paints of layers were mixed: wait until they will dry. Then apply paint again.

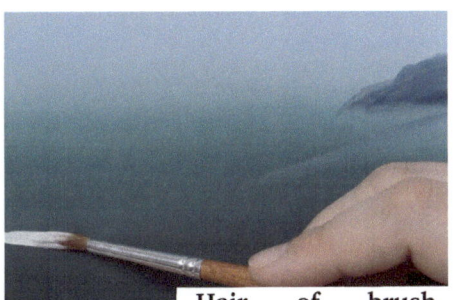

Hair of brush should be completely covered with paint.

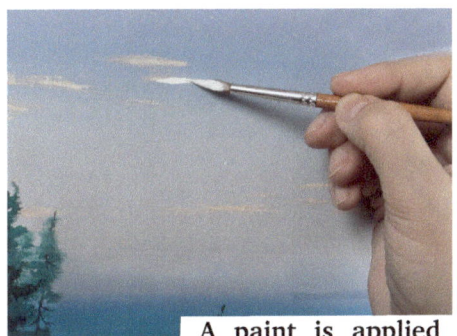

A paint is applied desirable in one stroke.

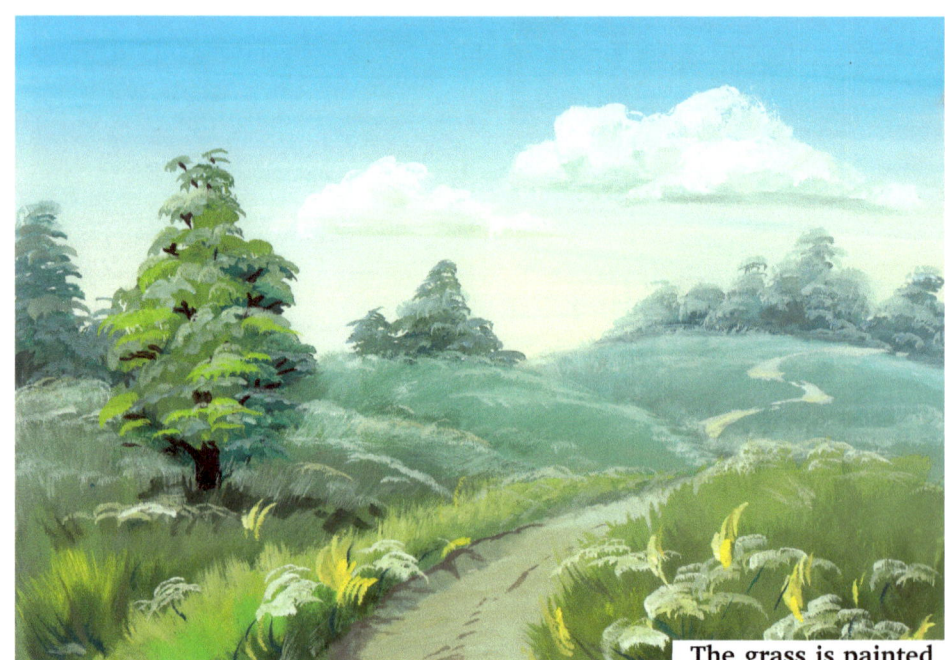

**The grass is painted with dry brush. Except wash and the grass, all the details were painted with a opaque layers.**

## Stages of Technique

1. Before applying the paint is thoroughly mixed on the palette. The mixture should is made with some reserve. Otherwise the paint will run out before the end work. Paint should be thick, and without lumps.

2. This quick technique, to paint of the bottom layer did not have time to dissolve. Helps to quickly paint the brush properly chosen size and shape. The desired area is painted with such the brush with a minimum of brushstrokes. On the brush should be a lot of paint.

3. The paint is applied with brush is moved at an acute angle to sheet. Strong pressing on the brush does not necessary. A paint is applied desirable in one stroke.

4. When paint is applied, need to pay attention to uniformity thick of layer. The thick layer of paint after drying can crack.

# Exercises

### Flowers – White and Yellow
Stain the sheet of paperboard with dark paint. Wait then it dries. Paint on stained sheet any white flowers with yellow middles.

### Clouds in The Sky
Take sheet stained with gradient like landscape: light-blue up and green bottom. Paint a light clouds on light-blue area. The result - a clouds in the sky.

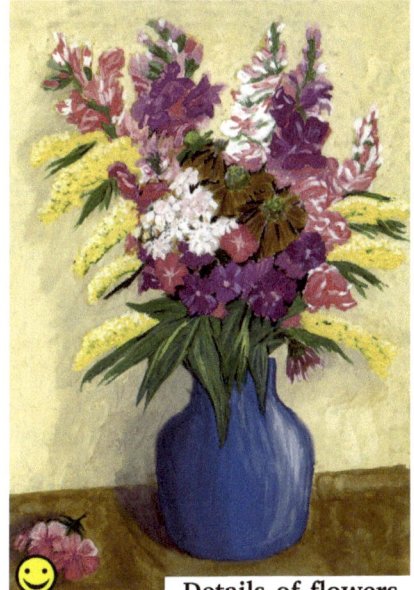

**Details of flowers and leaves were painted with the opaque layers.**

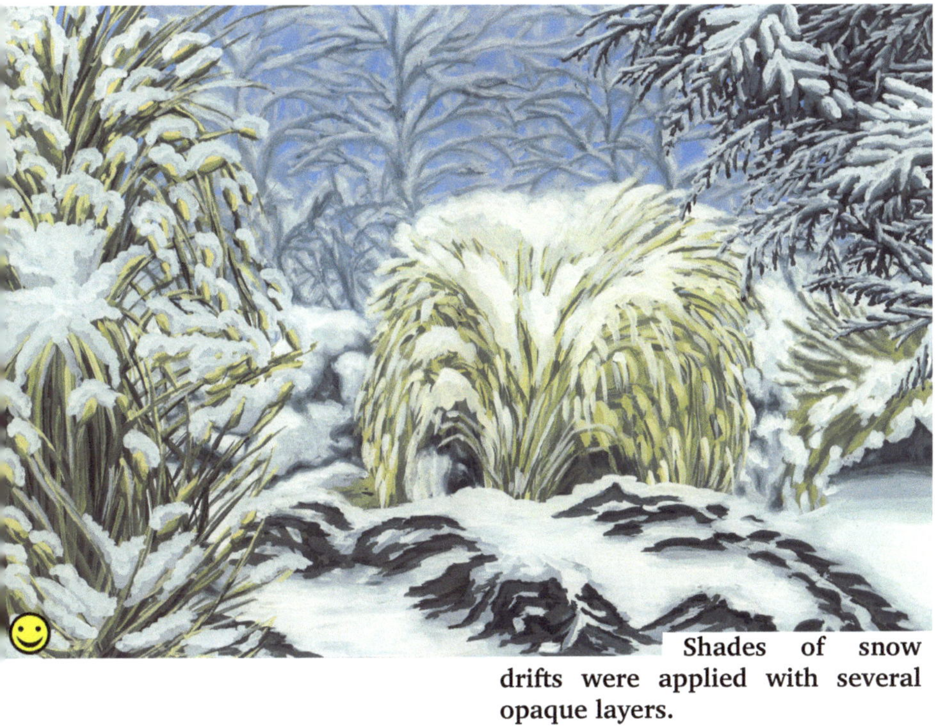

**Shades of snow drifts were applied with several opaque layers.**

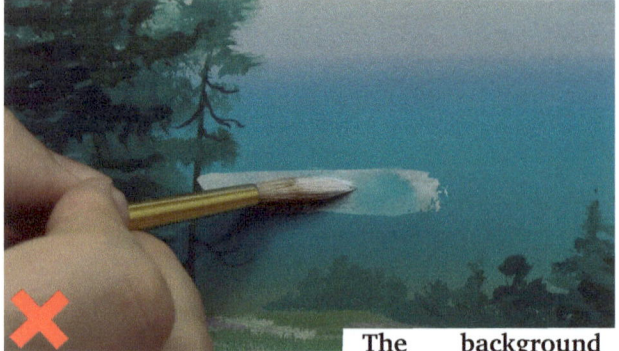

The background was dissolved with a lot of strokes. This does not opaque layer. This other technique - wash with paint.

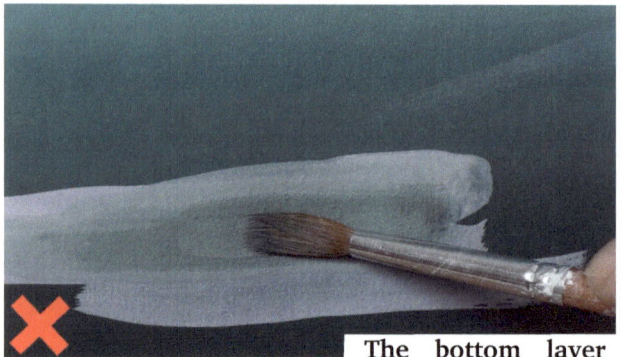

The bottom layer was dissolved because of too liquid paint.

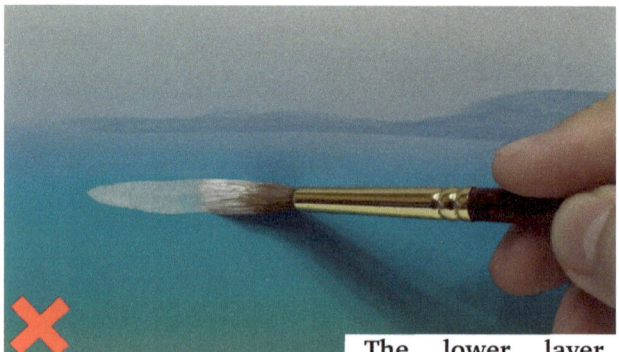

The lower layer was not overpaint, because the paint too liquid and transparent.

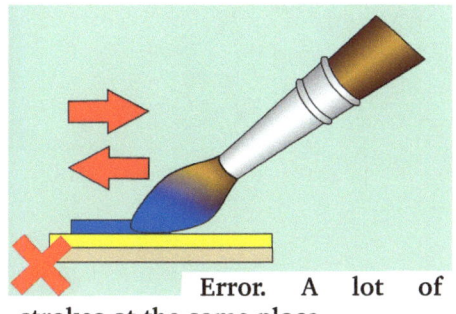

Error. A lot of strokes at the same place.

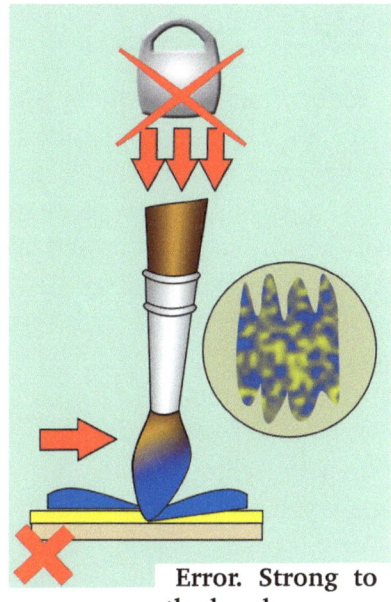

Error. Strong to pressure on the brush.

## Most Frequent Errors

Very little paint on the brush.
Very liquid paint.
Strong pressure on the brush.
A lot of strokes at the same place.

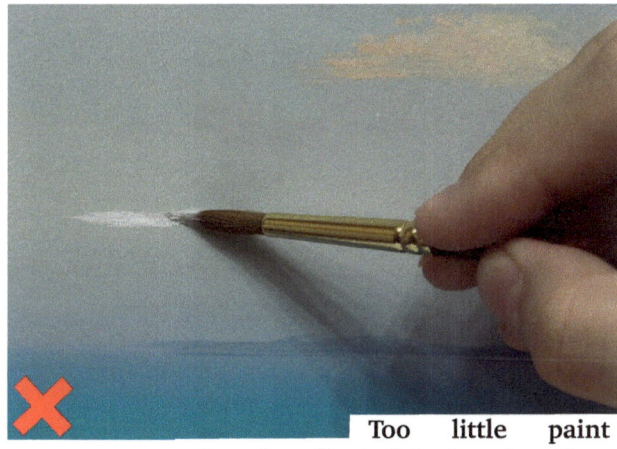

Too little paint gives the effect of dry brushwork.

# Helpful Tips

Yellow paint is semi-opaque. It can not completely hide dark background. Even if it is applied with thick layer. Blue background will be visible through and with a layer of yellow paint will create a green tint. How do paint yellow spot on blue background? Desired area of blue background overpainted with a white paint. When the paint will dry on white apply yellow.

If paint was laid down unevenly or with gaps: when paint will be dry, overpaint its again.

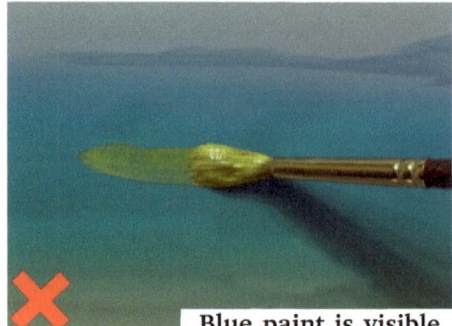

**Blue paint is visible through yellow layer.**

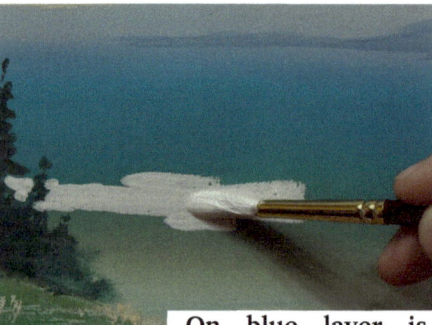

**On blue layer is applied opaque white.**

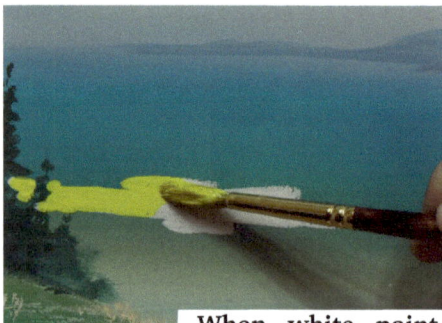

**When white paint will dry, it will be overpainted with yellow paint.**

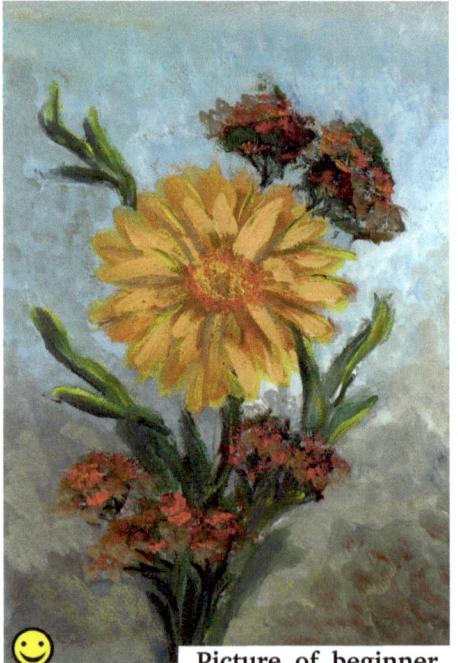

**Picture of beginner painter was painted with use opaque layers.**

# Compatibility with Other Techniques

Opaque layers can be used together with any techniques.

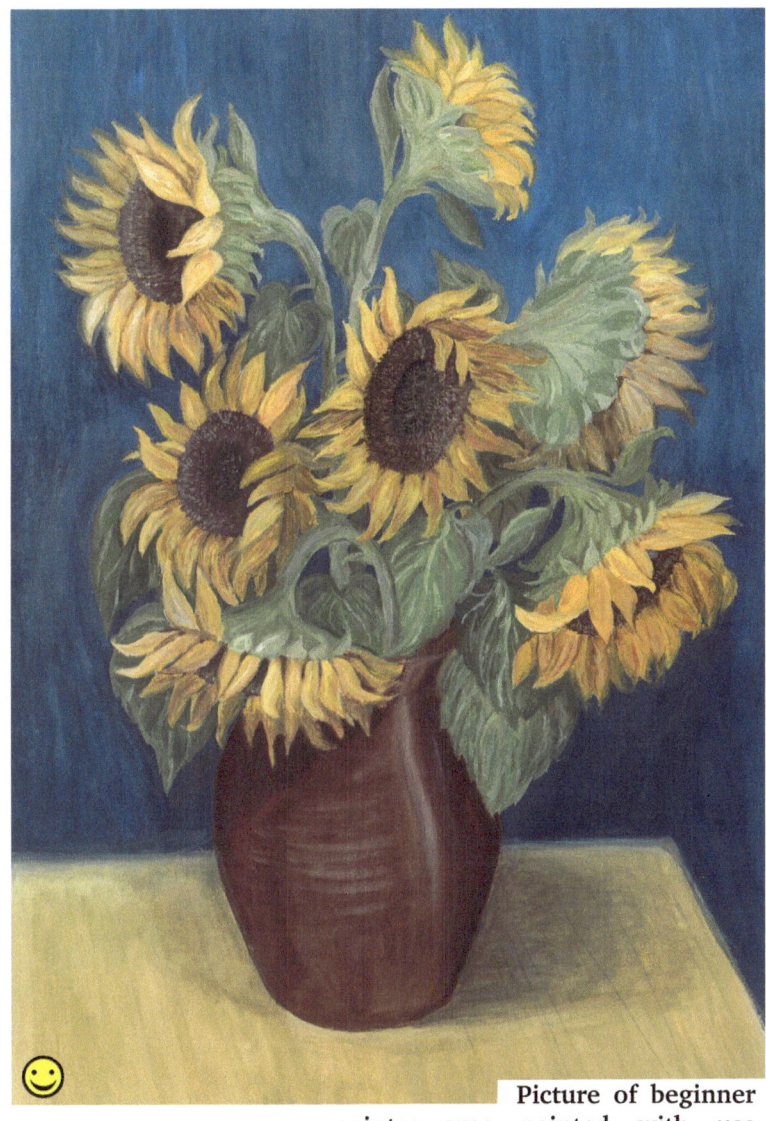

Picture of beginner painter was painted with use opaque layers.

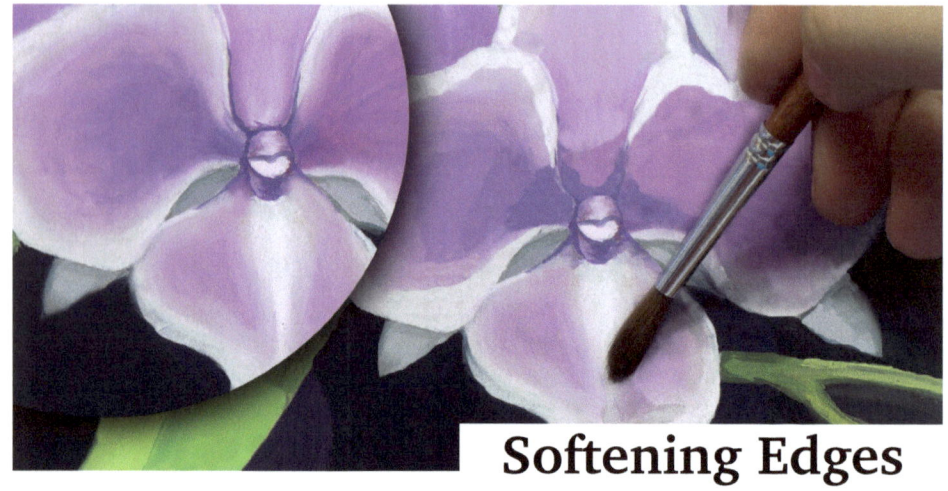

# Softening Edges

Softening edges is used for making gradient between color areas.

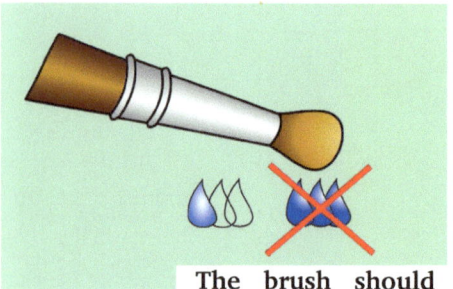

The brush should be clear and slightly damp.

Softening edges do not wash color areas (as wash with water or paint). The technique of softening edges only blend borders between adjacent colors.

The gradient effect between colors is formed with blending border of dry color areas with damp brush.

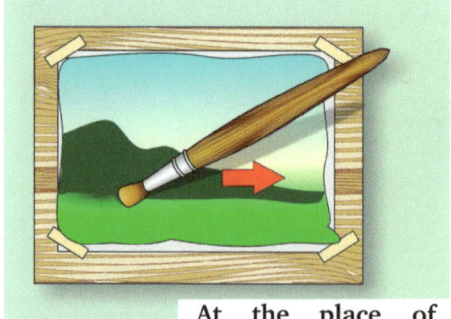

At the place of softening edges is used one-way moving of the brush.

Softening edges of color areas like a mini-wash. This technique is used for small details of picture. The wash is used for making large gradient area.

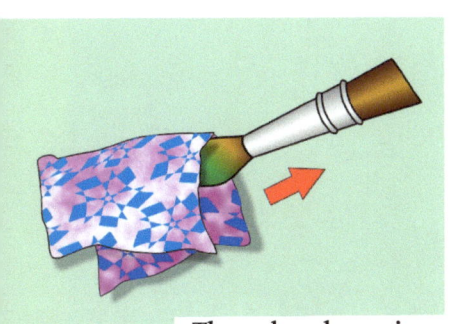

The brush wipe with rag. Hairs of brush like spatula.

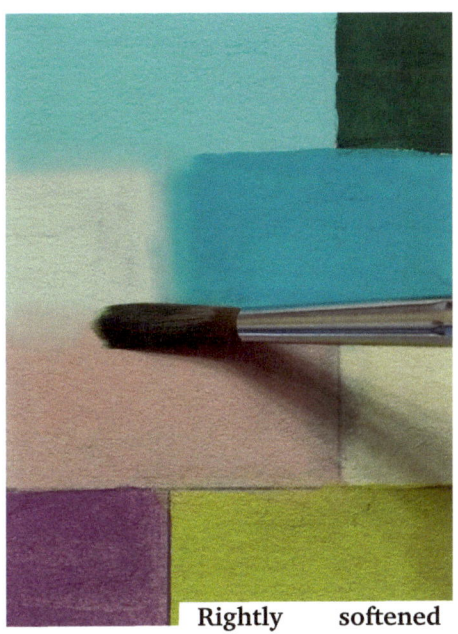

Rightly softened edges.

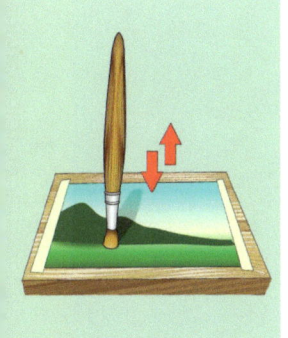

Softening edges can with stippling. Clean, damp brush with easy tapping on border between colors.

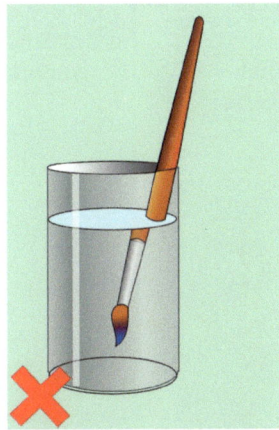

The brush will be not cleaned if its will not be rubed on the bottom.

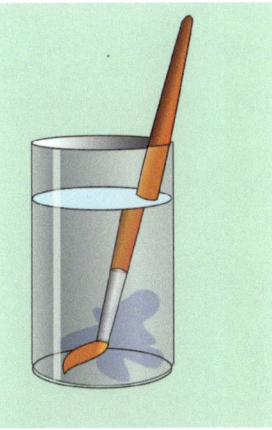

The brush is thoroughly washed. Hairs of brush is rubed on the bottom.

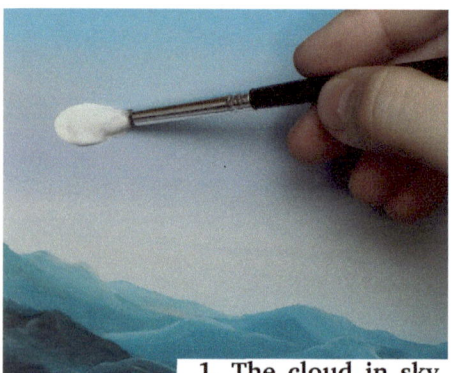

1. The cloud in sky was painted with thick paint.

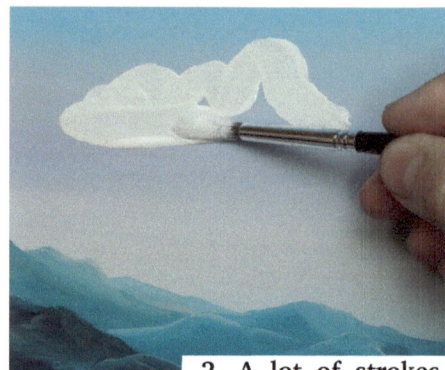

2. A lot of strokes on the same place do do not necessary. Otherwise lower layer will be blended with the upper.

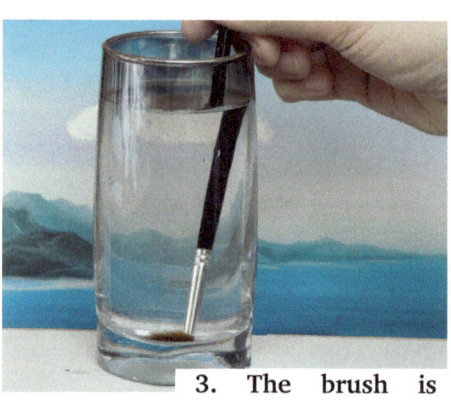

3. The brush is thoroughly washed in clear water.

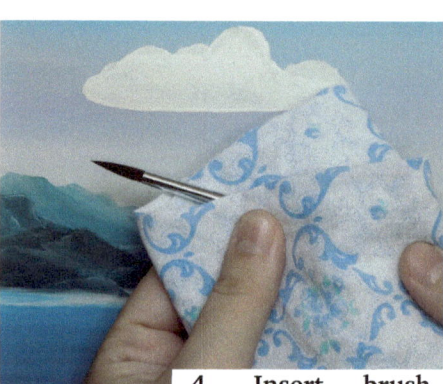

4. Insert brush between layers of cloth.

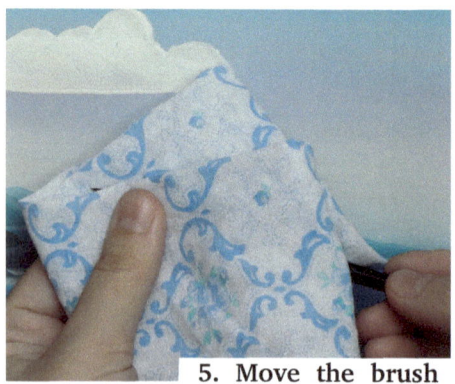

5. Move the brush forward shaft.

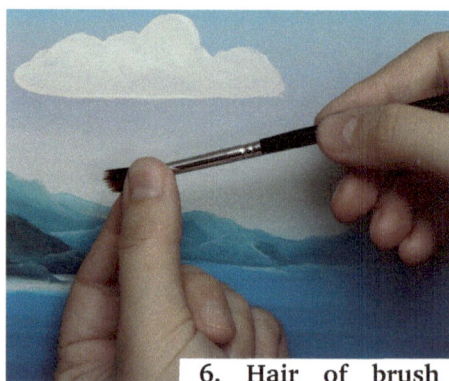

6. Hair of brush was squeezed. Now the brush like spatula.

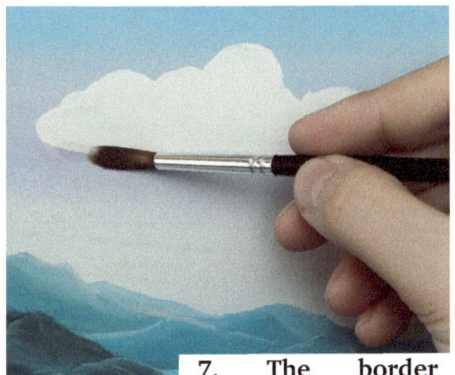

7. The border between colors is blured with the "spatula".

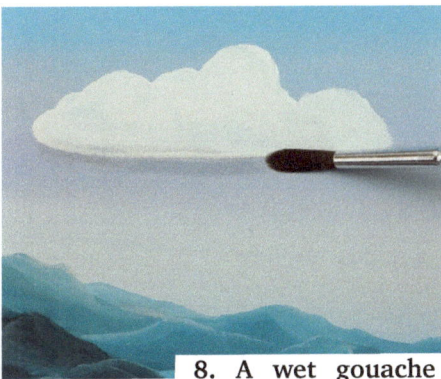

8. A wet gouache paint darker than dry.

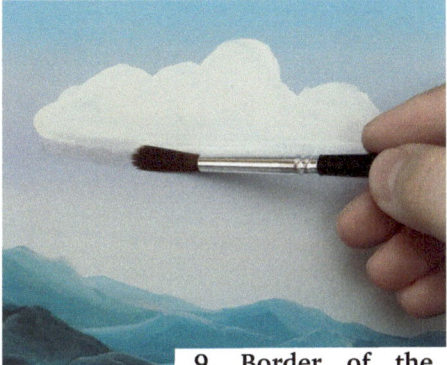

9. Border of the cloud is blured with repeated movements of the brush.

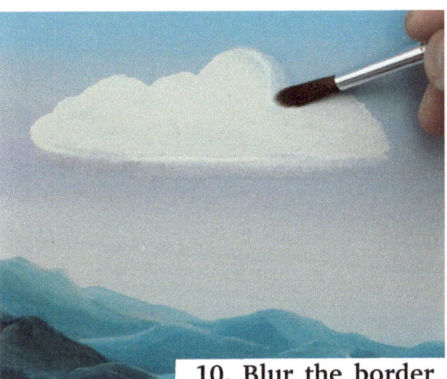

10. Blur the border of bottom of cloud and of a few other places.

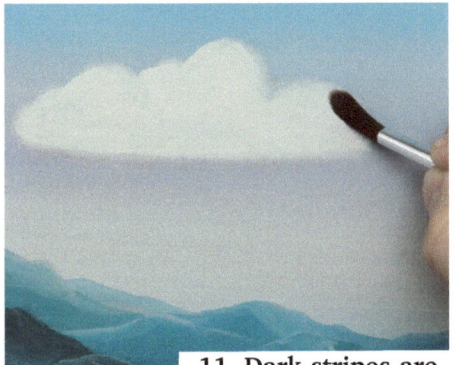

11. Dark stripes are visible because the paint is wet.

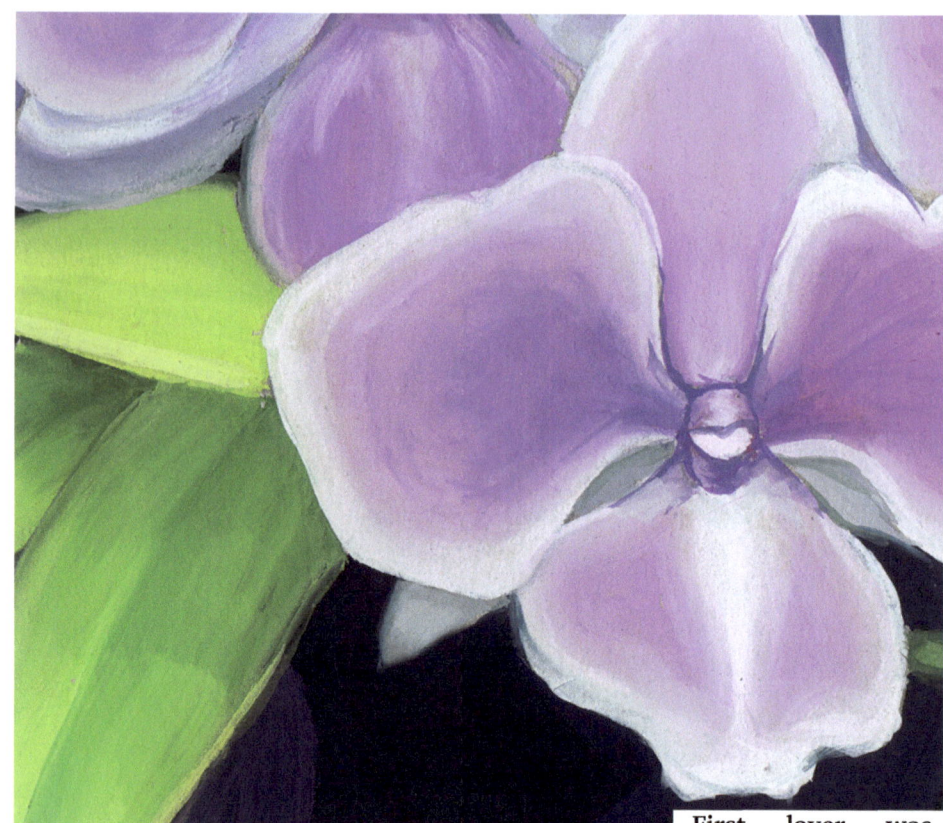

**First layer was applied with uniform staining. Smooth gradations between white and purple colors was painted with softening edges.**

## Stages of Tehnique

1. Wait when paint will dry.

2. Wash a brush in clear water. After wash: wipe the brush with rag. Squeeze with fingers hairs of brush, so that they become like spatula. That "spatula" is used for softening edges. The brush should be slightly damp, but no wet. Do not use very dry brush. Otherwise it will leave strips.

3. At the place of softening edges the brush is moved one-way. The brush should move at an acute angle and hardly touches the surface. Otherwise the paint will be picked up with brush.

4. Do not rotate the brush. Otherwise colors will not be in place.

# Exercises

## Colors Bands

Take sheet 10X15 cm (4x6 inch). Apply on the sheet two brushstrokes: dark and light. Wait until they will dry. Make several strokes on the border two colors with a clean and damp brush. The brush should hardly touches sheet, and move in the same direction. If colors were mixed and at place their border band of mixture: can use softening edges to borders of band of mixture.

## Clouds

Make gradient wash at dark-blue and light-blue colors. This will be like sky if painted clouds.

Clouds is painted with white with admixture ocher. The paint should apply quickly. Otherwise a upper and a lower layers will be blended.

Soften edges of a bottom and some other parts of clouds. Make blurring different width.

Don't wash the brush! Paint a few spots at clouds closer to the edges, with the same brush. Apply at clouds a few spots with white. Blur edges of white spots. Be careful. Otherwise upper and lower layers will be blended.

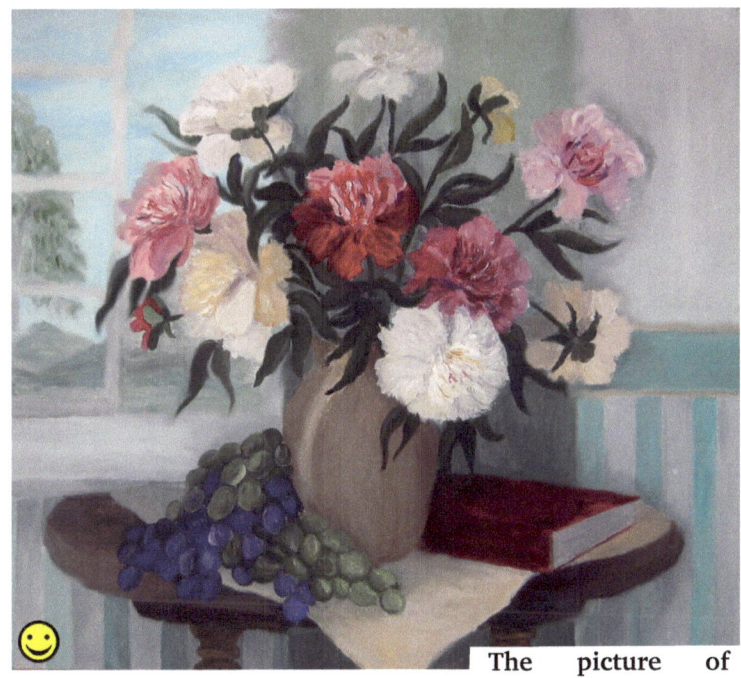

The picture of beginner painter was painted with use of softening edges.

# Most Frequent Errors

The lot of strokes with brush at the same place.

The poorly washed brush.

The brush is used very wet or very dry.

A very thin layer of paint at the place of softening edges.

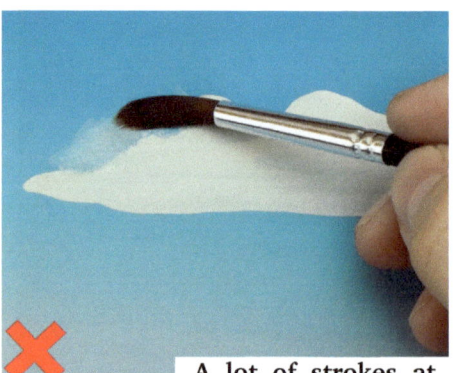

A lot of strokes at the same place. The result - layers of paint are dissolved and blended.

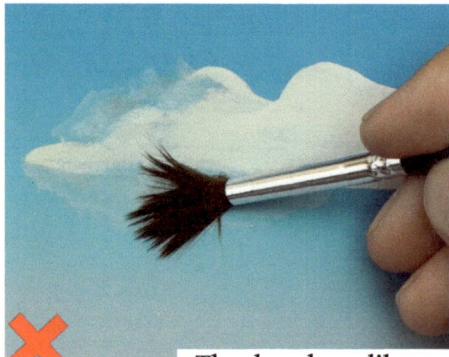

The brush unlike a spatula. And also the brush does not at acute angle to the sheet.

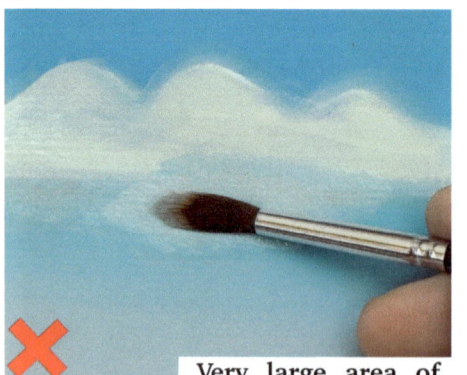

Very large area of softening edges and blurred all boundary between strokes.

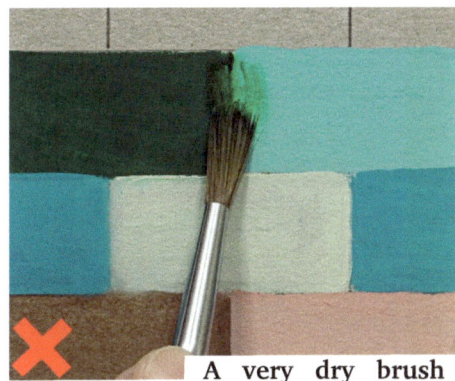

A very dry brush will leave traces like a lot of strips.

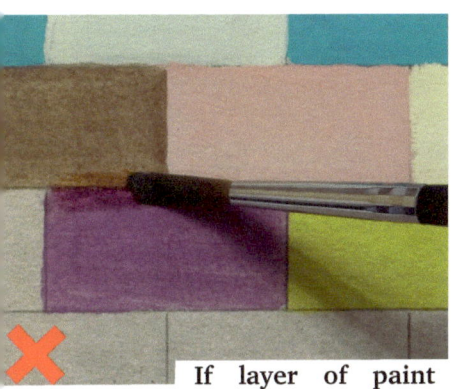

If layer of paint thin and transparent, softening edges will not be.

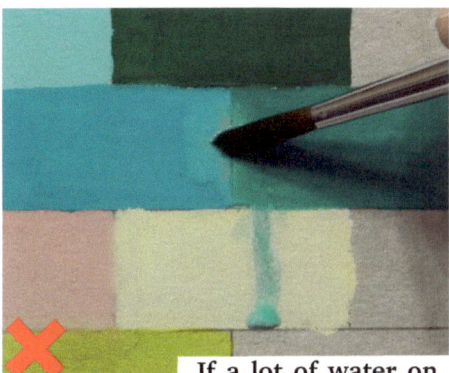

If a lot of water on a brush, then paint will be dissolved. Paperboard will visible through semi-opaque layer.

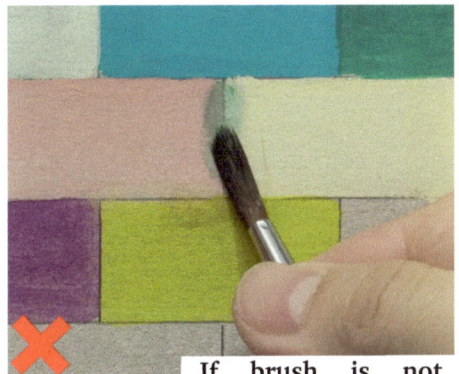

Long work with brush at the same place gives mixed colors.

If brush is not carefully washed, it can leave traces of paint.

# Helpful Tips

For softening edges used not only soft-hair brushes, but also bristle brushes. Bristle brushes leaves behind stripes. This will very good look in surrounded of brushstrokes dry brushwork. The bristle brush is not used for smooth gradients.

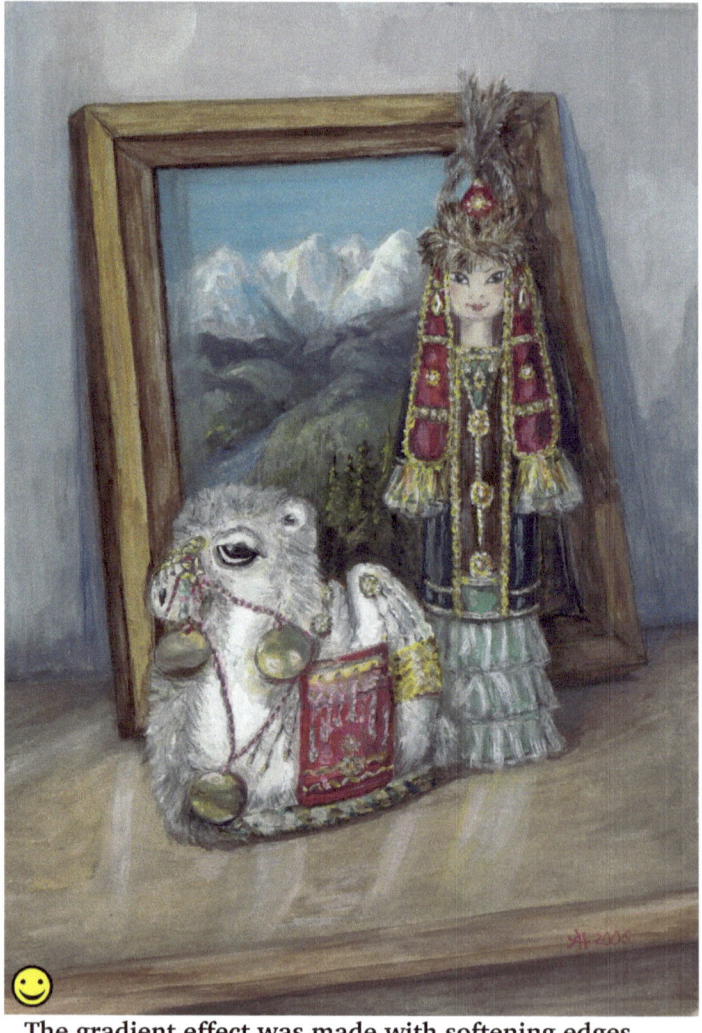

**The gradient effect was made with softening edges.**

## Compatibility with Other Techniques

Softening edges can be used together with any techniques, except: stamping, liquid gouache first layer, spattering

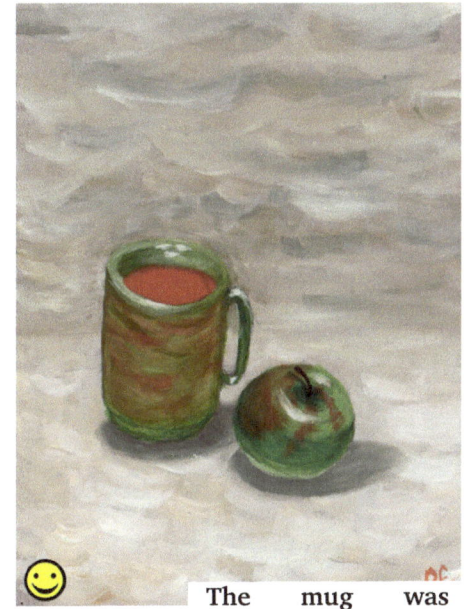

The mug was painted with use of softening edges.

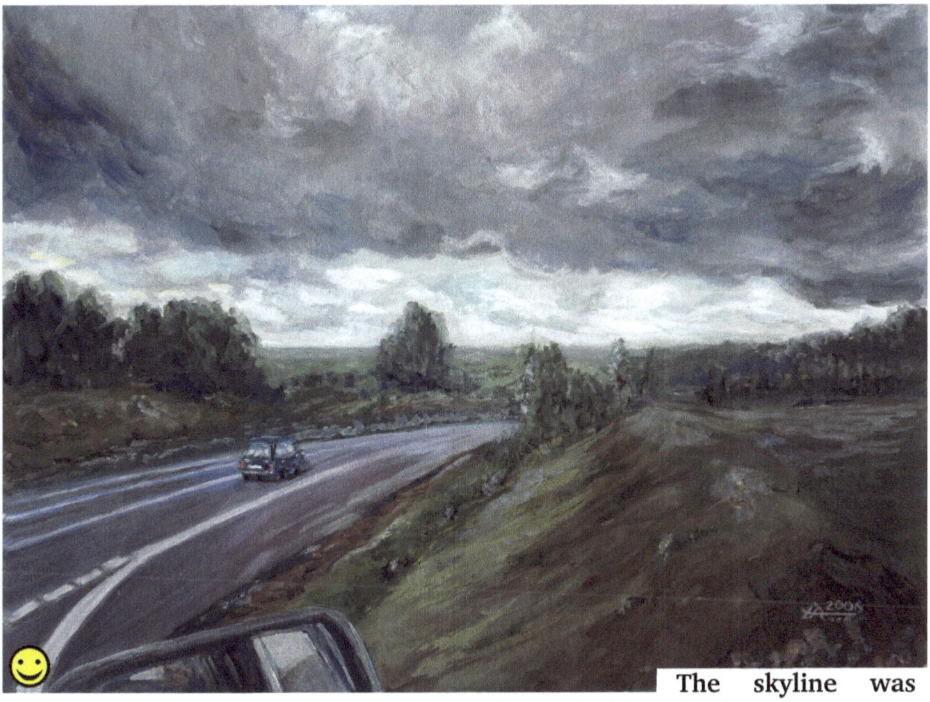

The skyline was blurred with softening edges.

# Still Life with Jug

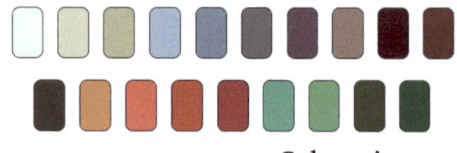

Color mixtures

Used techniques: opaque layers, uniform staining, softening edges.

The picture painted at sheet 21x19 cm (8 1/4x7 1/2 in). With self-painting can take anywhere from 4 to 5 hours.

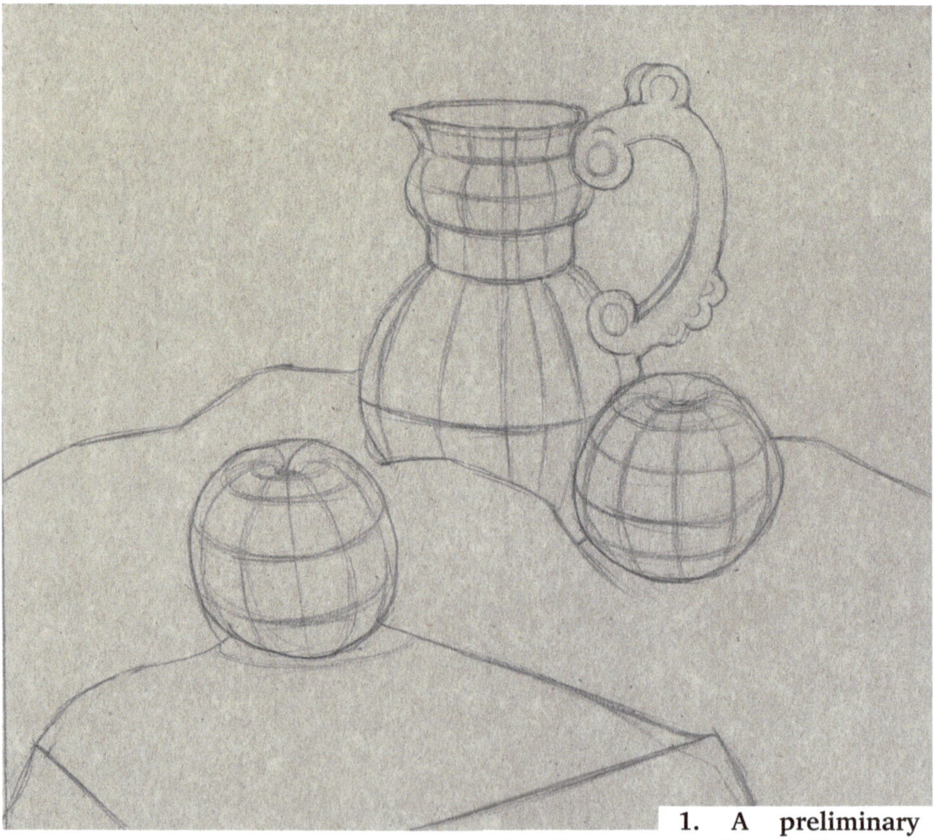

1. A preliminary drawing was done in pencil.

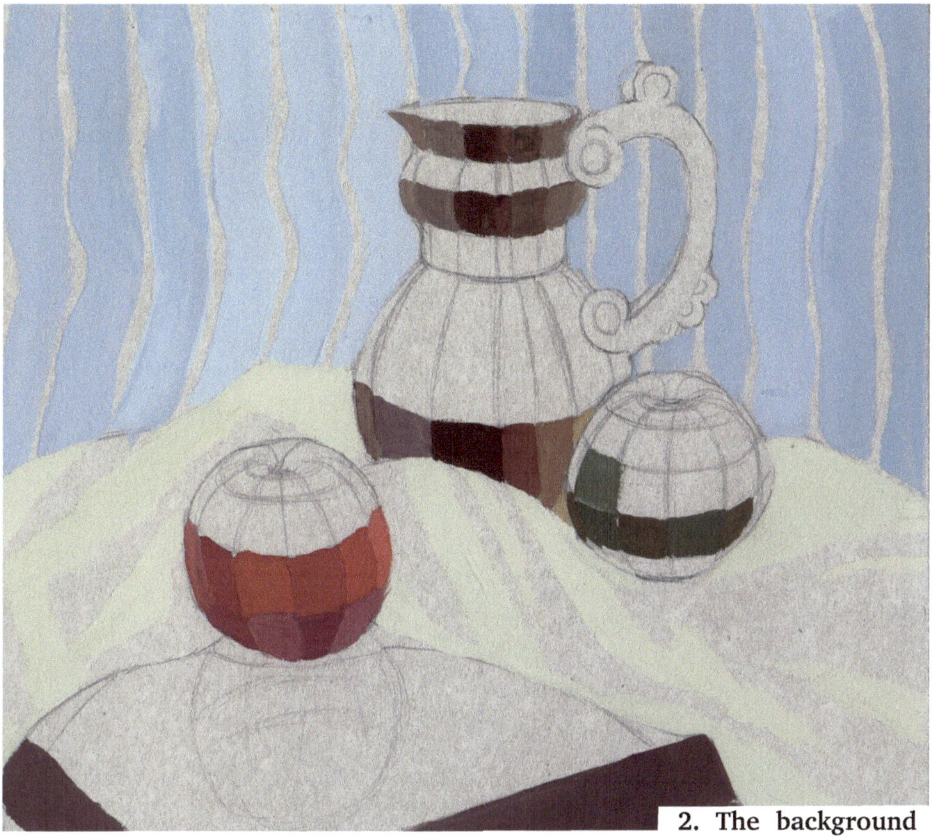

**2. The background was created with use a uniform staining.**

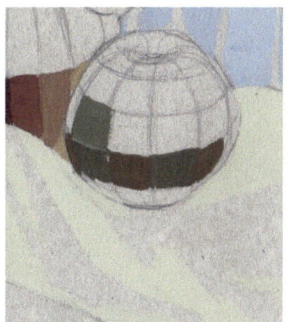

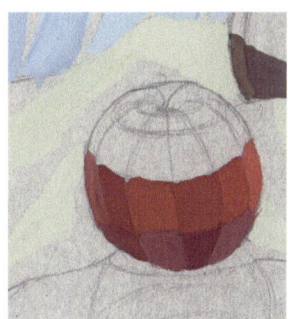

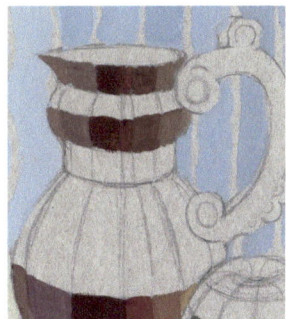

Each fragment of apple's image was stained with their shade. Tones of each fragment differ from other.

The penumbra's area and shadow's area of drapery were stained with the same mixture of colors.

A few fragments of the same color were painted at the same time.

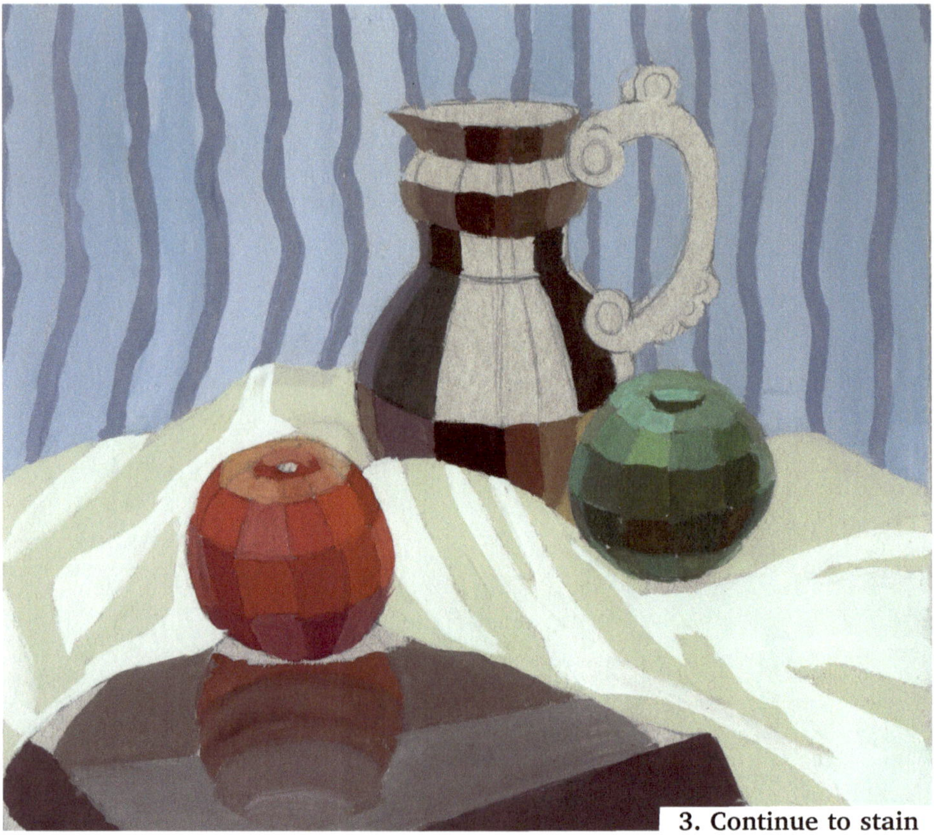

**3. Continue to stain fragments of all objects of still life.**

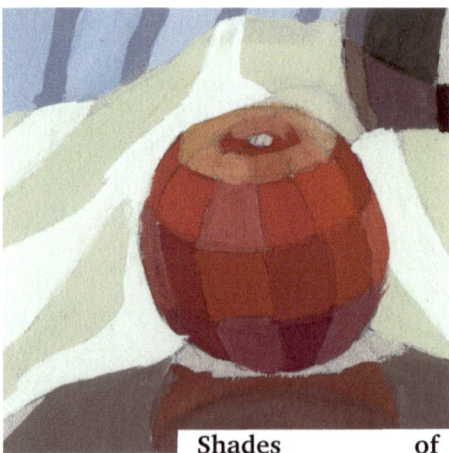

**Shades             of fragments should be most diverse. Apple's reflection was stained.**

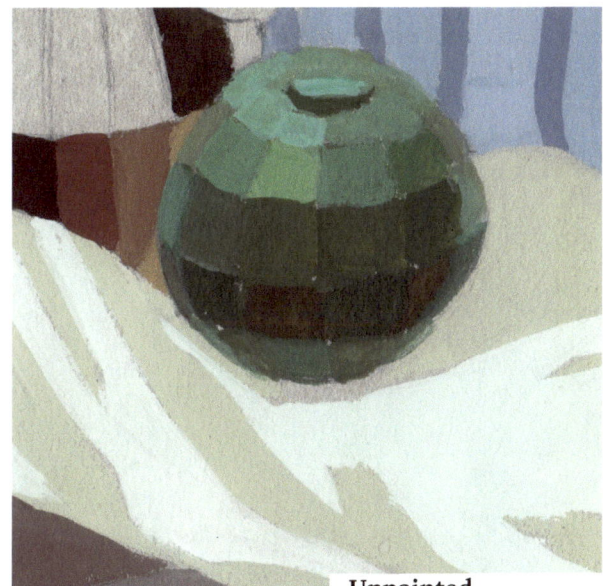

Unpainted fragments of drapery were painted with the color mixture of light.

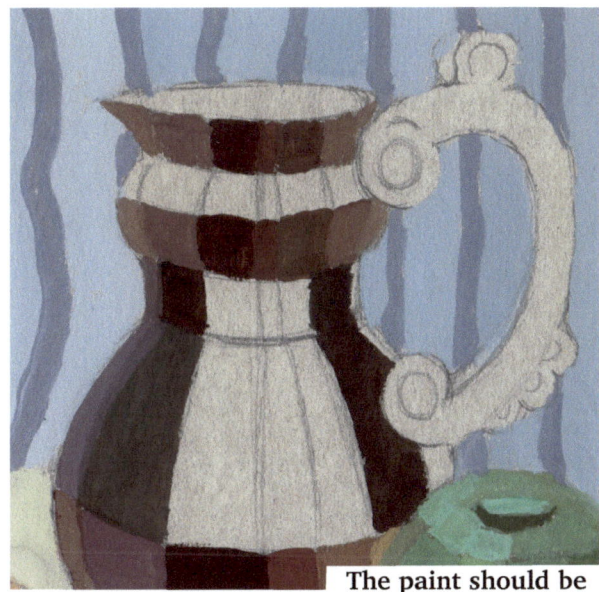

The paint should be thick, so paperboard not visible through the layer of paint. This especially important for mixtures of brown color.

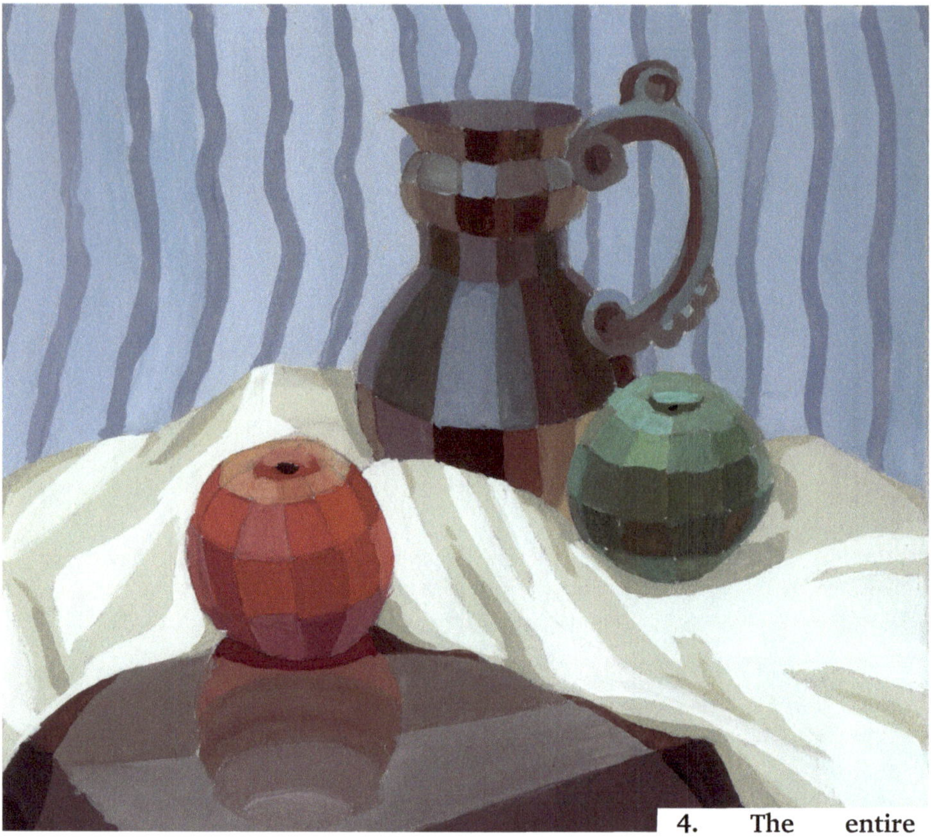

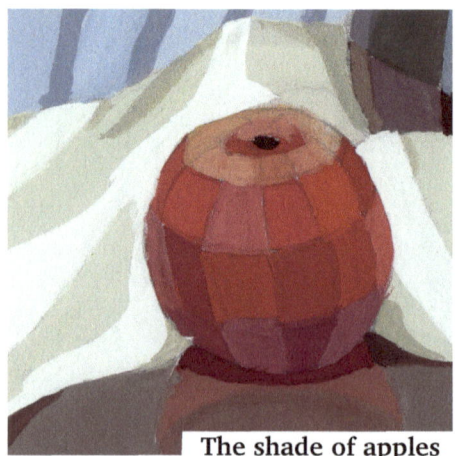

**4.	The	entire canvas was stained.**

The shade of apples
and draperies were painted.

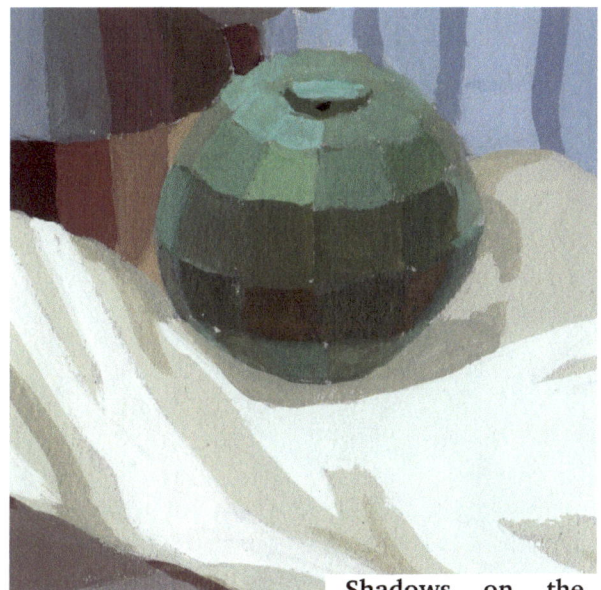

Shadows on the drapery were painted with opaque layers.

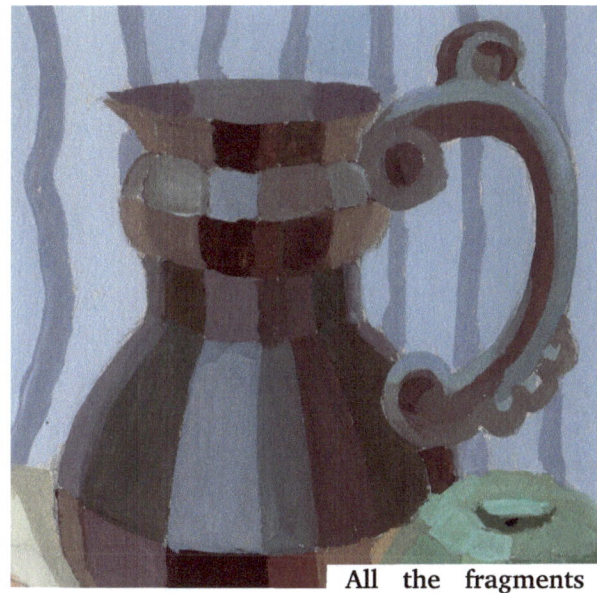

All the fragments were uniformly stained. Light on the handle of a jug was painted with technique opaque layers.

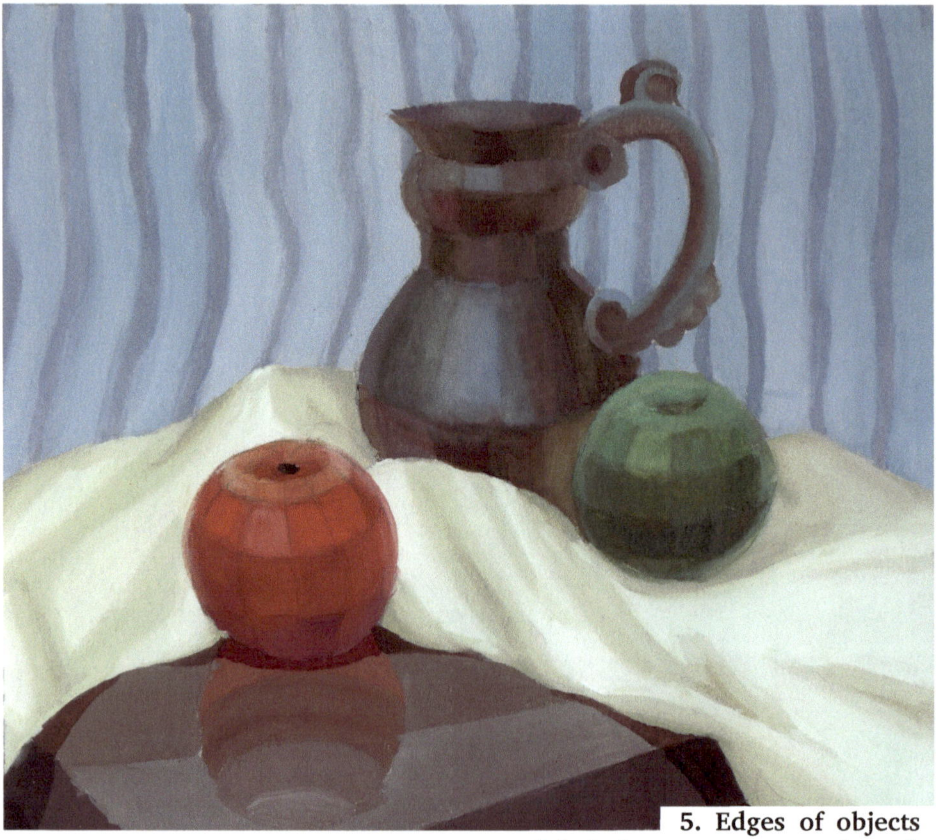

**5. Edges of objects and their fragments were softened, except the table and the jug.**

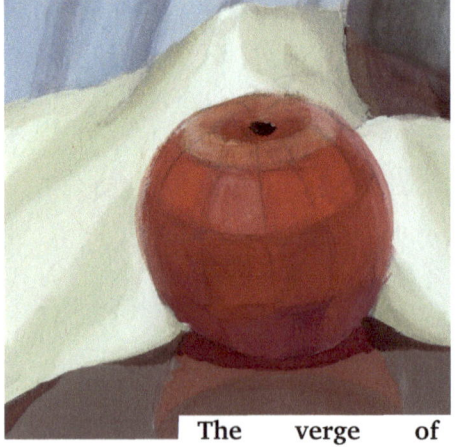

The verge of lighting still visible.

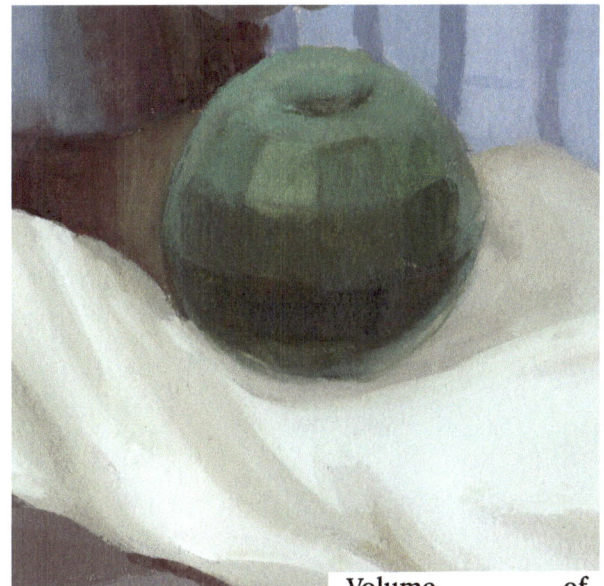

Volume of draperies was made with use softening edges.

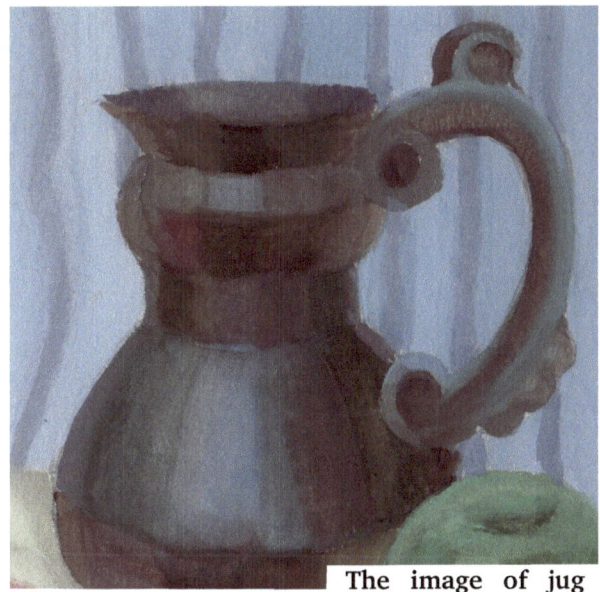

The image of jug became more realistic after use softening edges.

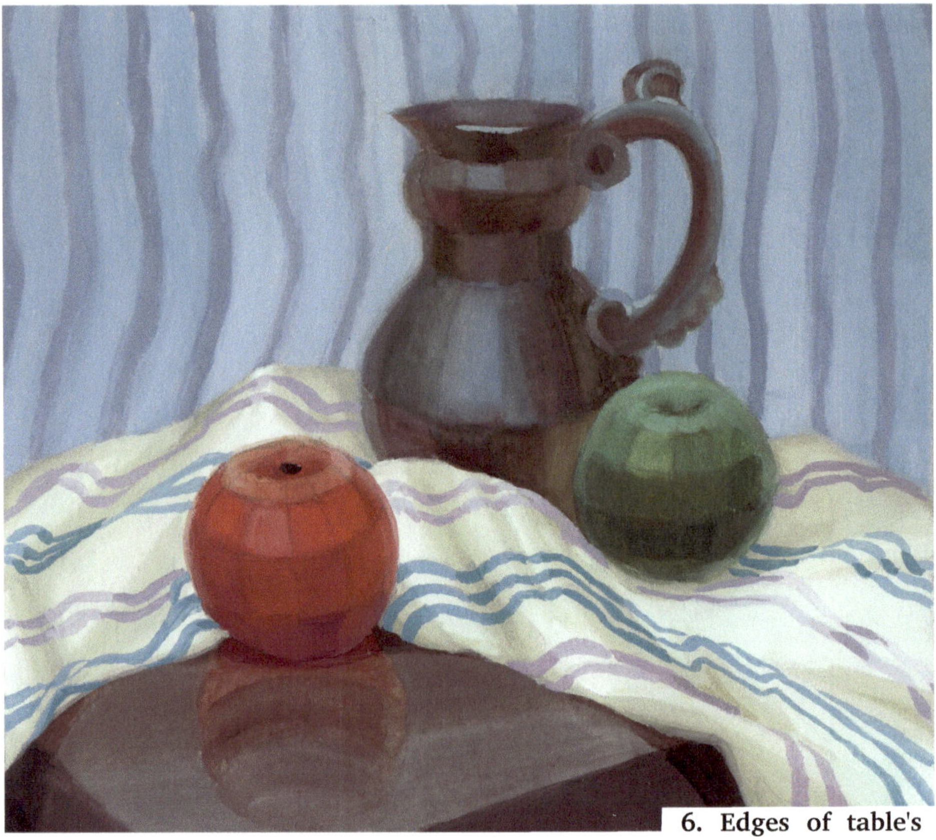

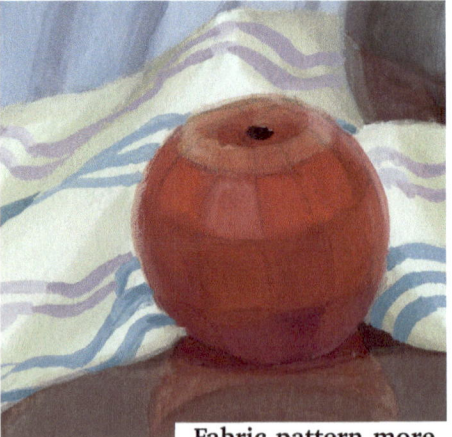

**6.** Edges of table's fragments were softened. On drapery were painted stripes.

Fabric pattern more convenient paint on the volume drapery.

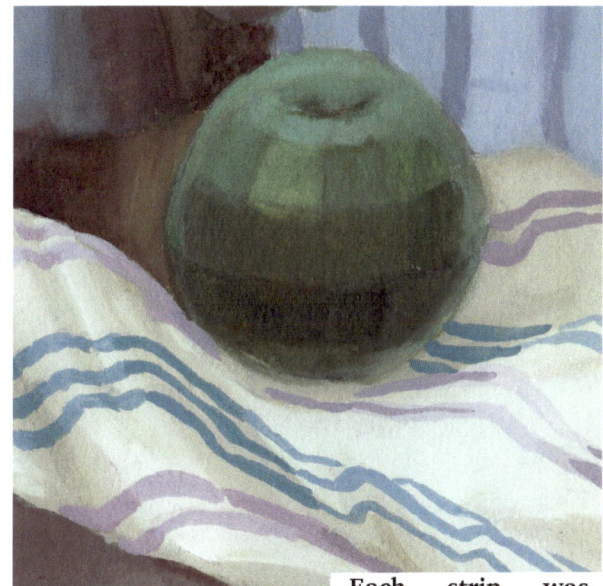

Each strip was painted with two color mixtures: for the shadow and light.

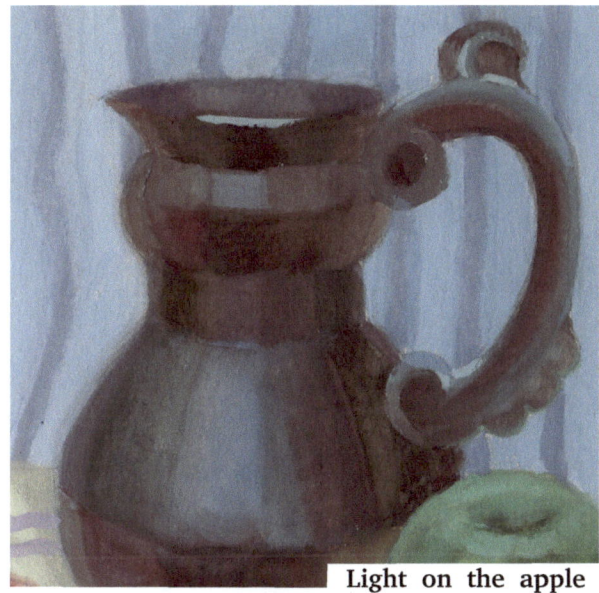

Light on the apple and the glare on the jug were painted with opaque layers.

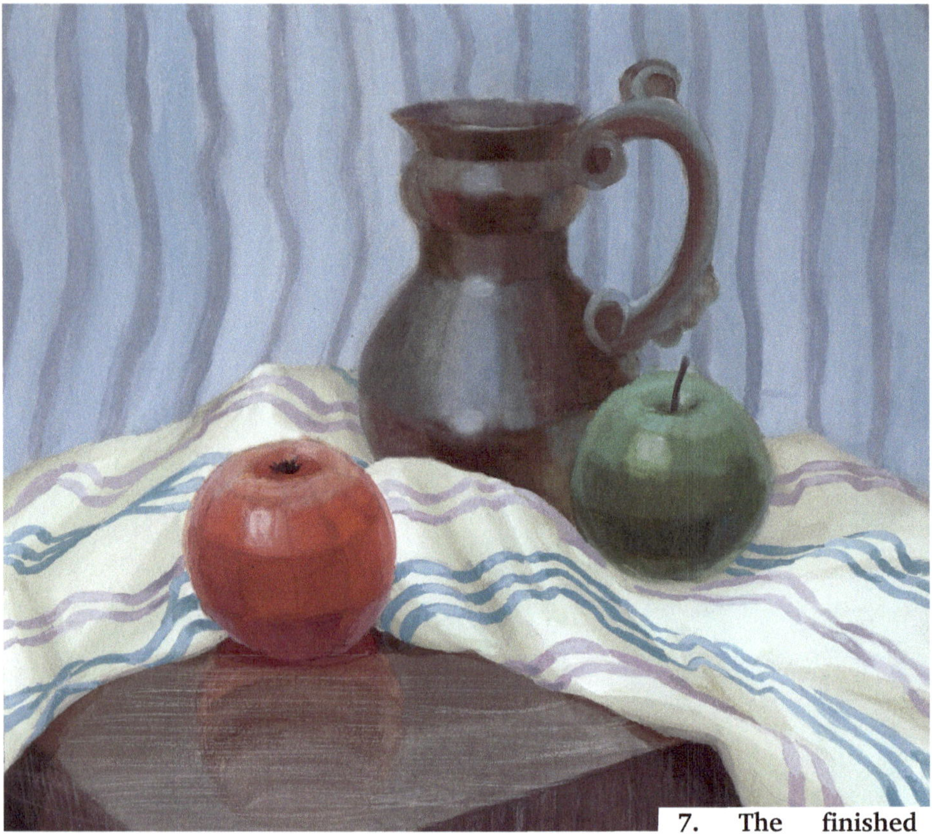

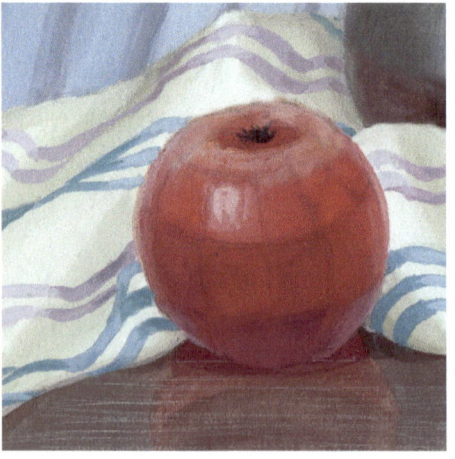

7. The finished picture was made with use of techniques: uniform color, opaque layers, softening edges.

Glare and light on the apple were painted with opaque layer and softening edges. Horizontal stripes on the table were painted with fine lines. This makes the table more realistic. Horizontal strips paint do not necessary.

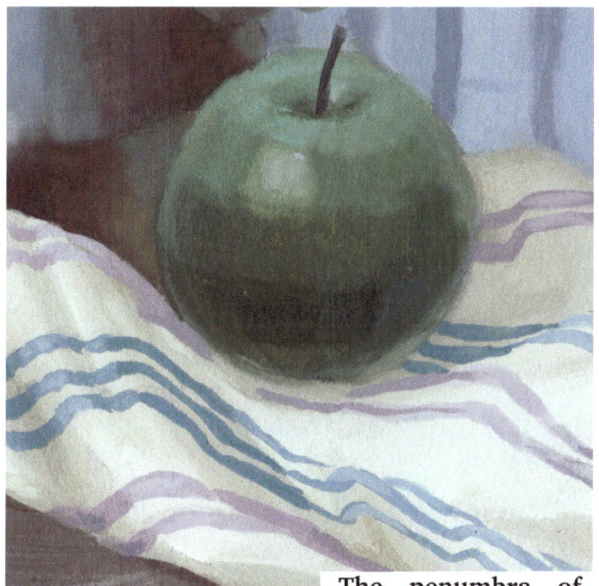

The penumbra of draping's strips was painted with softening edges. The glare and light on the apple were painted with opaque layer and softening edges. A tail of the apple was painted.

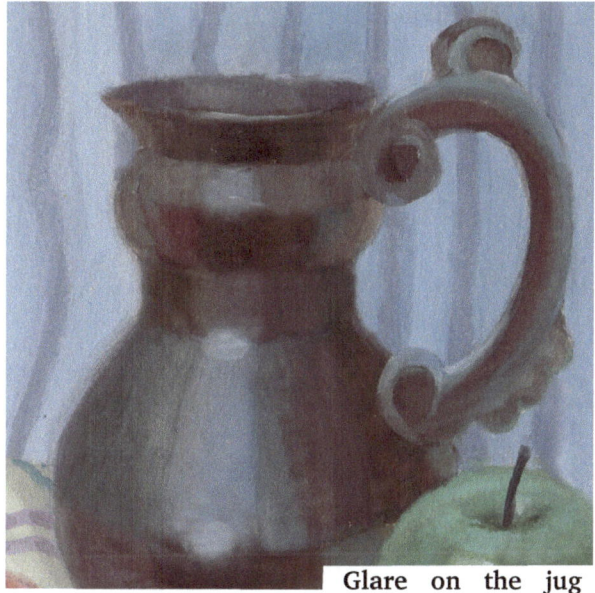

Glare on the jug was painted with opaque layer and softening edges. If the paperboard visible through a layer of paint: on fragments of semi-opaque layers are applied another layer of paint, then used the softening edges.

# Rose

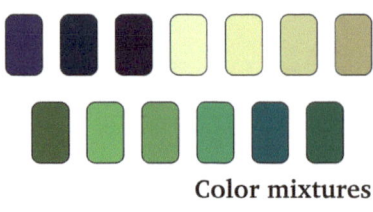

layers, uniform staining, softening edges.

The picture painted at sheet 21x19 cm (8 1/4x7 1/2 in). With self-painting can take anywhere from 4 to 5 hours.

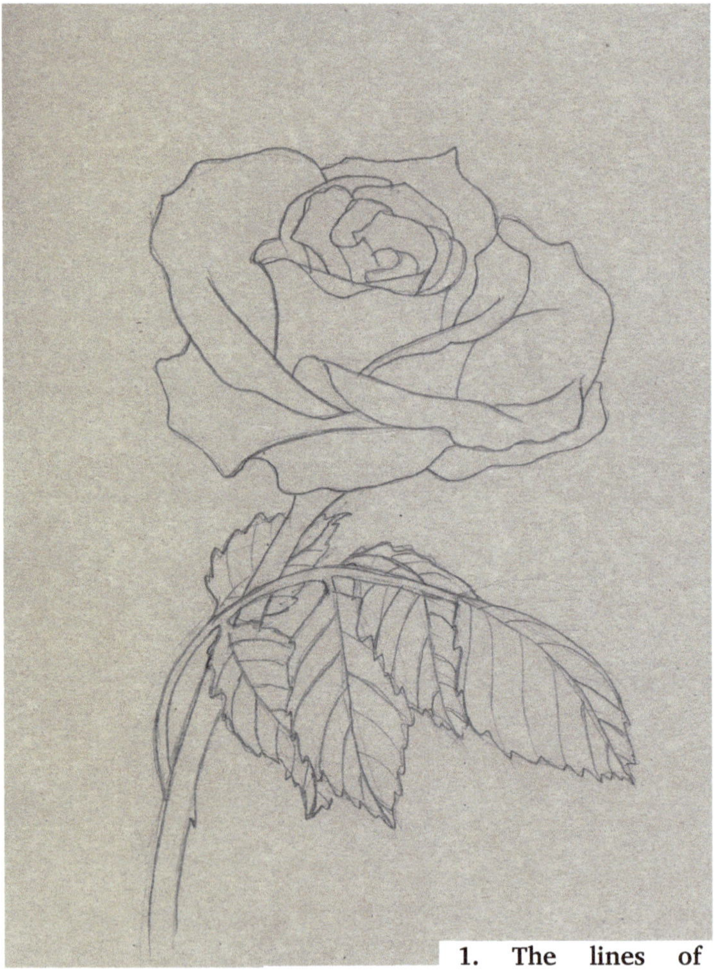

1. The lines of drawing were made bold for better visibility. Such bold lines in practice are not required.

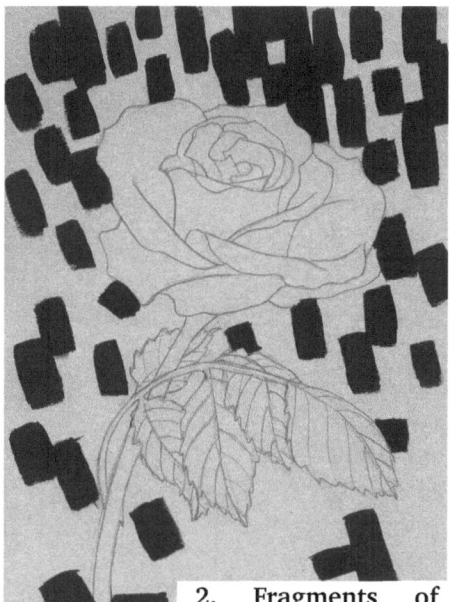

2. Fragments of background were painted with mixture black and green colors. The color mixture for background is need to create before start. Desirable to test the mixture on a separate sheet. The flat brush most convenient for paint this background.

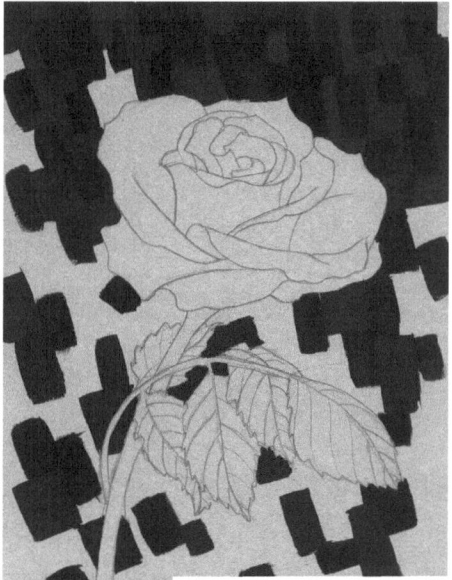

3. Fragments of background were painted with mixture black and colors. The border of the rose should be carefully painted.

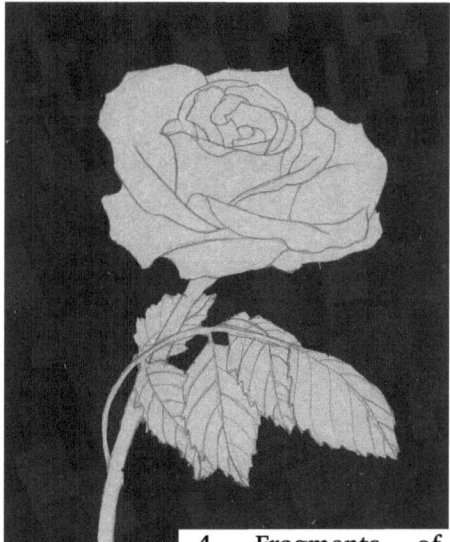

4. Fragments of background were painted with mixture green-black and violet-black colors. Gaps between colored areas should not be.

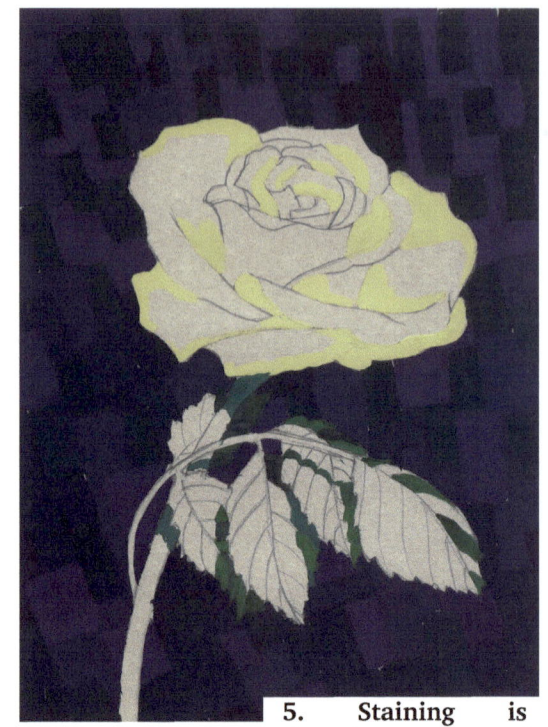

**5.** Staining is started from the dark areas of flowers and leaves.

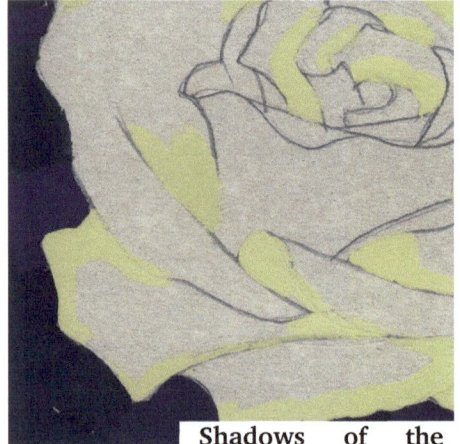

Shadows of the flower were pained with mixture of white, ocher, black and blue colors. Pencil lines should be overlaid with paint.

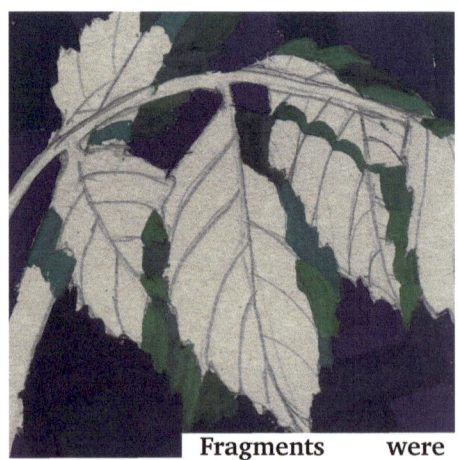

Fragments were painted of different shades of green and blue.

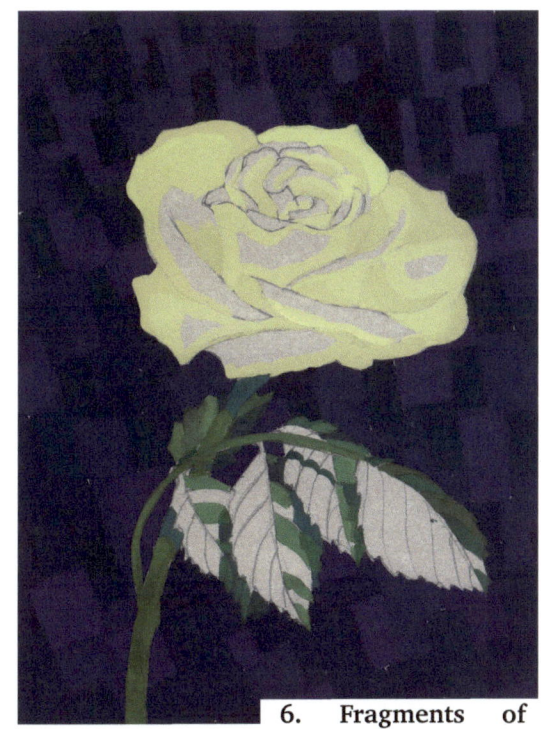

6. Fragments of leaves, stems and flowers were painted with a lighter color.

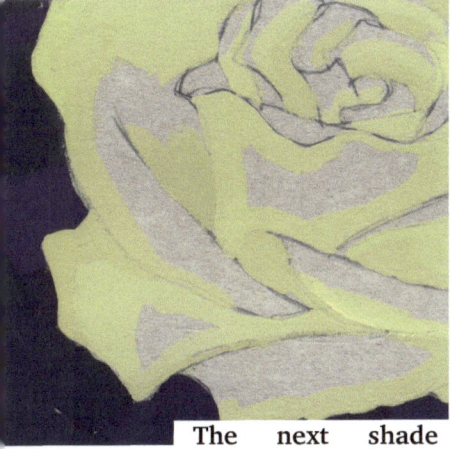

The next shade should be lighter than the previous one.

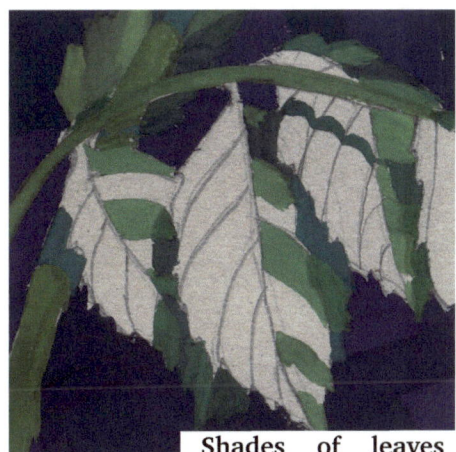

Shades of leaves should be more green and less blue.

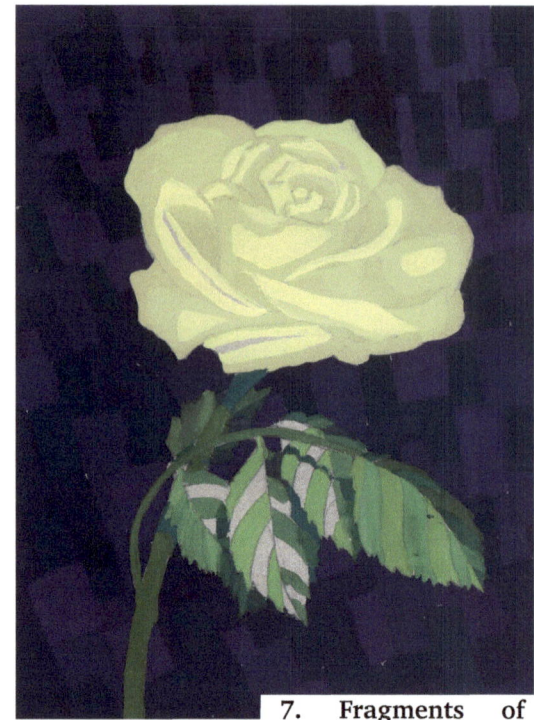

7. Fragments of flower and leaves were painted with light paint.

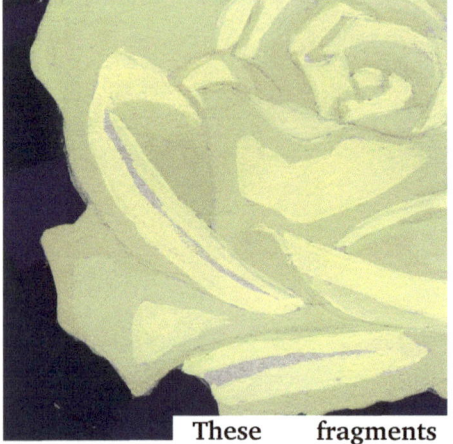

These fragments were painted with mixture of white and ocher with a small addition of yellow colors. Only lightest areas were left unpainted.

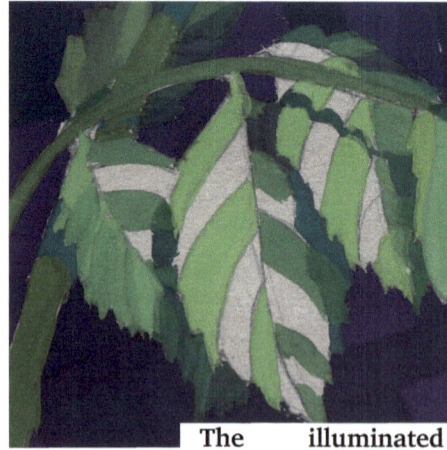

The illuminated part of leaves was painted with a mixture of green and yellow colors.

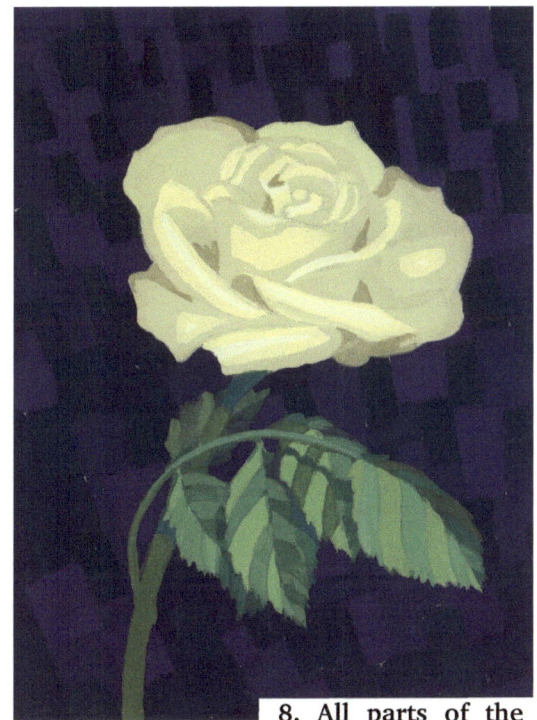

8. All parts of the picture are completely painted.

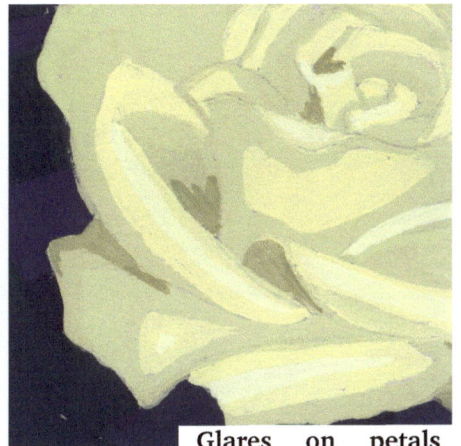

Glares on petals were painted with a mixture white and ocher colors. Shadows were deepened with thick layer of mixture of white, ocher, brown, blue and black colors.

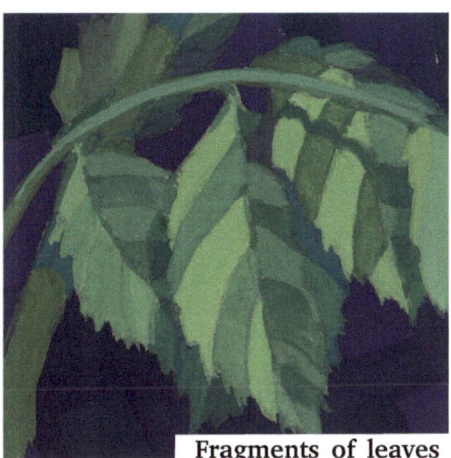

Fragments of leaves were painted with a shade of green.

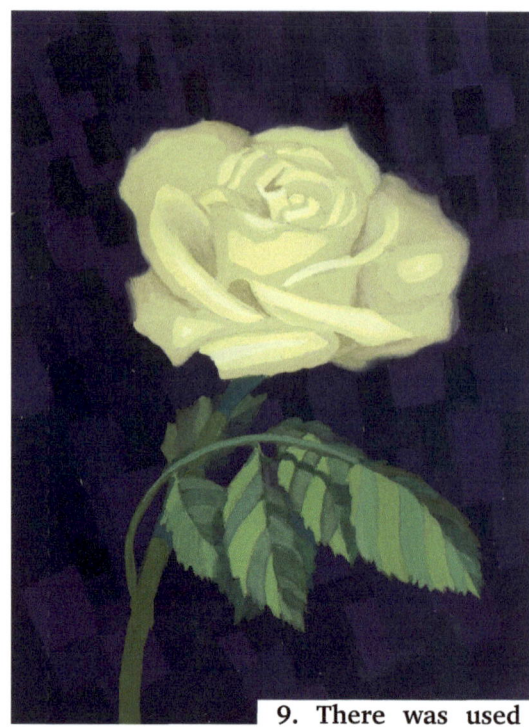

9. There was used technique softening edges.

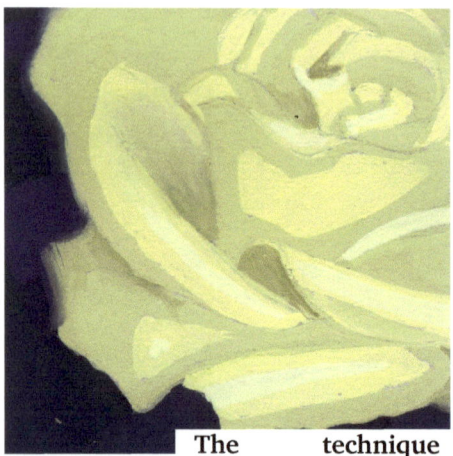

The technique softening edges was used: between shadow and penumbra of the flower, and on far edge of the flower.

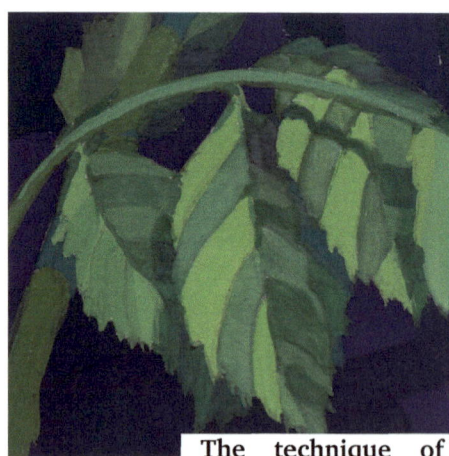

The technique of softening edges was used to paint shadow of leaves.

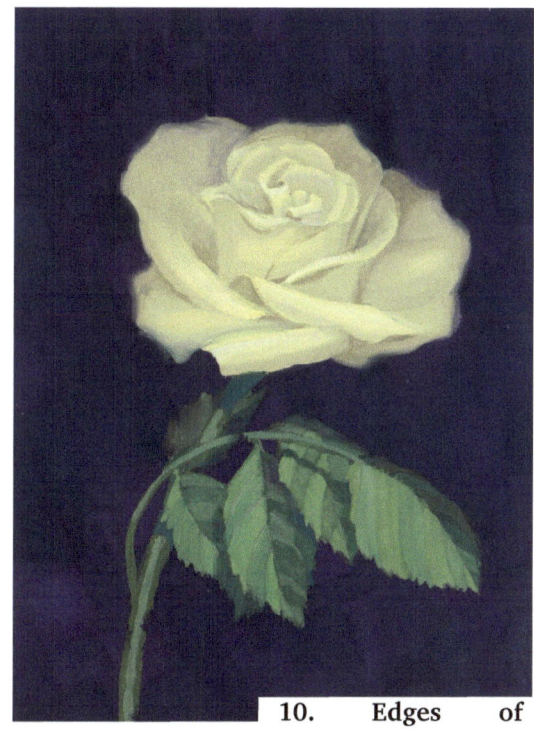

10. Edges of background's fragments and distant fragments of leaves were softened with wide soft-hair brush.

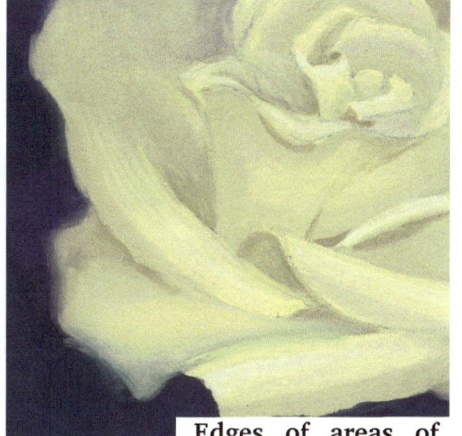

Edges of areas of penumbra and light were softened. If the shape of the petals is broken, then it can be restored with use apply thick paint over them.

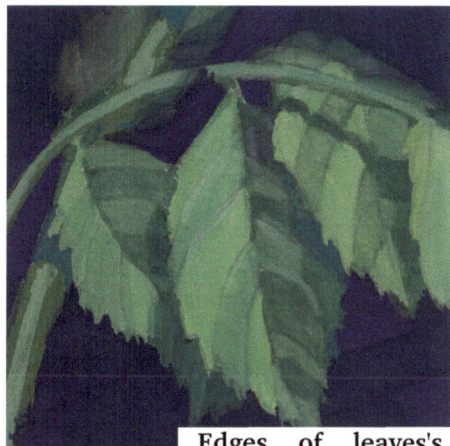

Edges of leaves's areas of light were softened. Opaque layer of paint was applied on the light's area of stem.

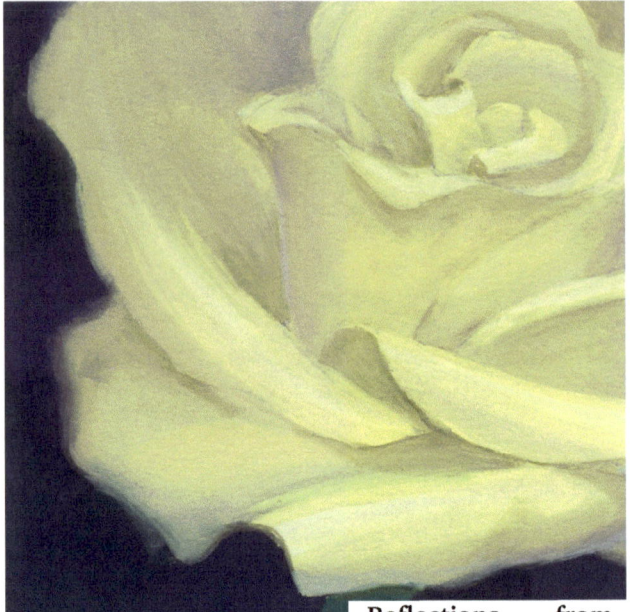

Reflections from violet background was applied with opaque paint. Edges of reflections were softened.

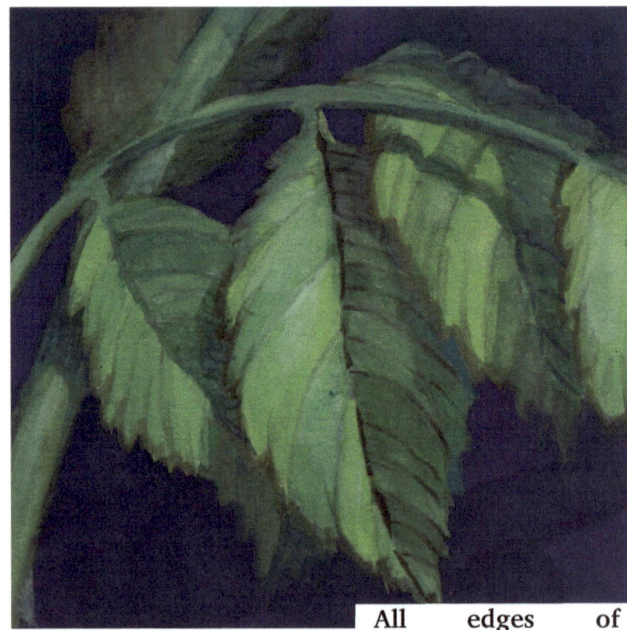

All edges of fragments of the stem were blurred. Streaks were painted with technique of fine lines.

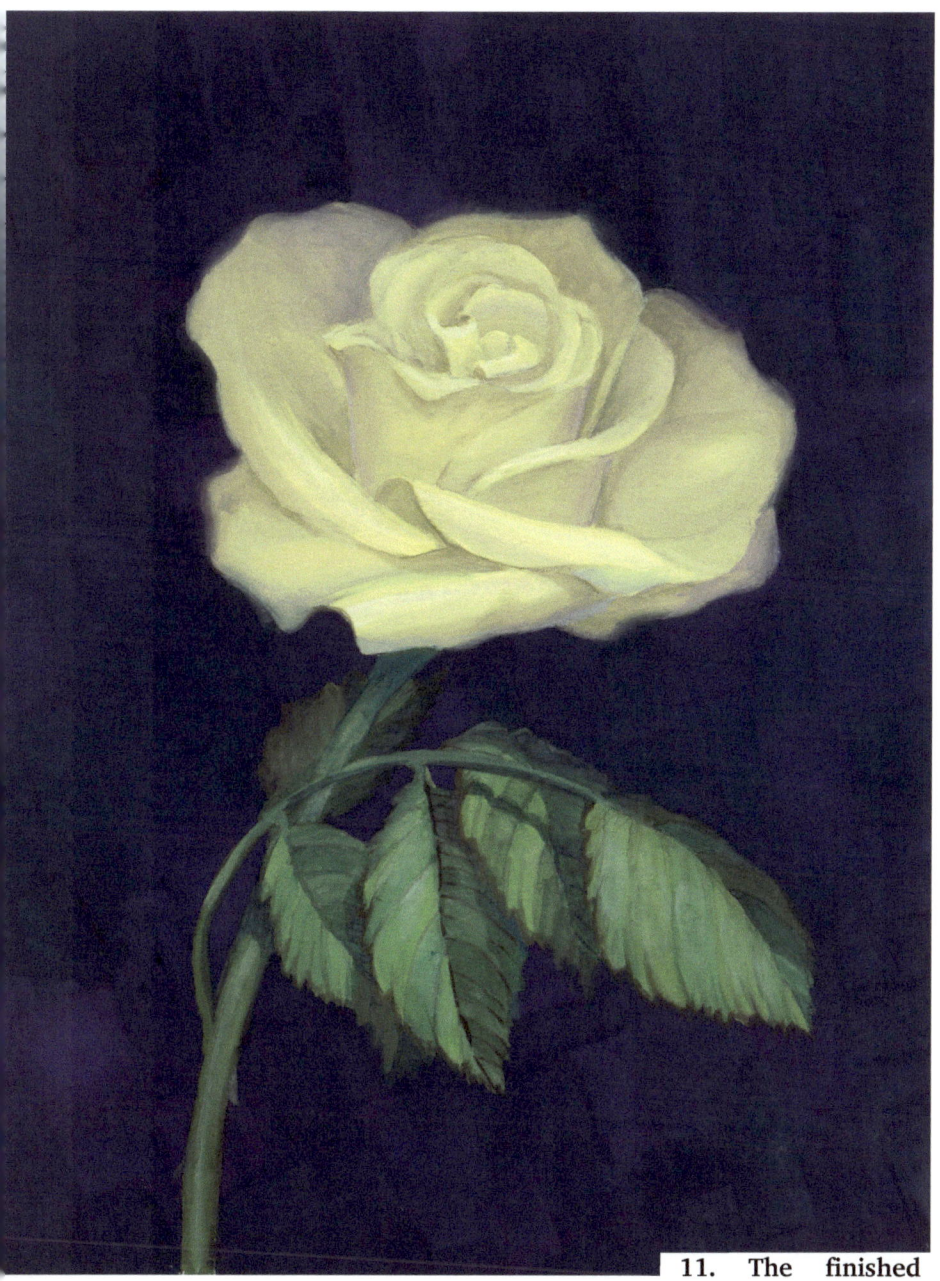

**11. The finished picture.** All edges of areas were softened. Streaks on leaves were added.

# Summary of All The Volumes Techniques Gouache Painting

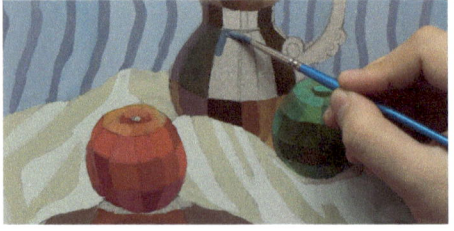

## Uniform Staining
Uniform Staining is used for overlaying support with uniformly and thin paints layer.

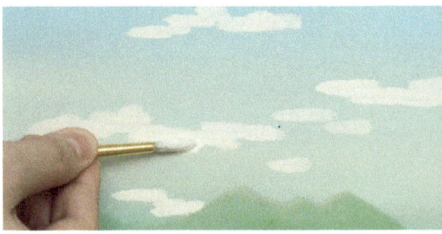

## Opaque Layers
Opaque Layers are used to hide a bottom layers.

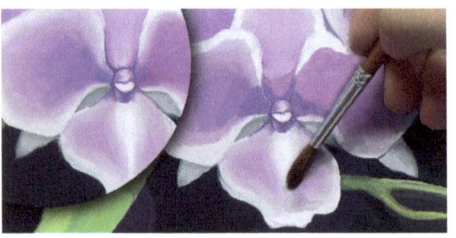

## Softening Edges
Softening edges use for make gradient between brushstrokes.

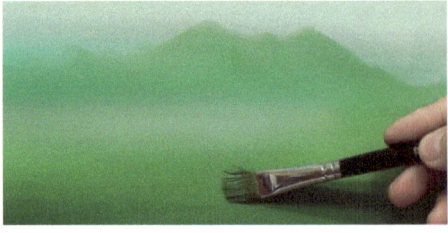

## Gradient Washing
Color gradient to large area is making with technique Gradient Washing.

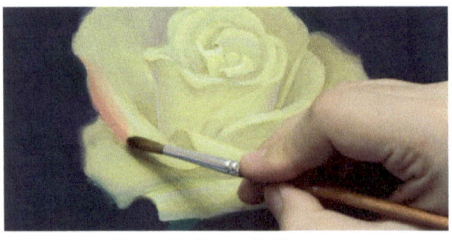

## Gouache Liquid
Technique Gouache Liquid is applied for painting semi-opaque layers and fine detail.

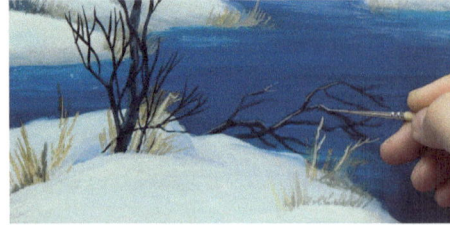

## Fine Lines
This technique used for painting fine lines with gouache.

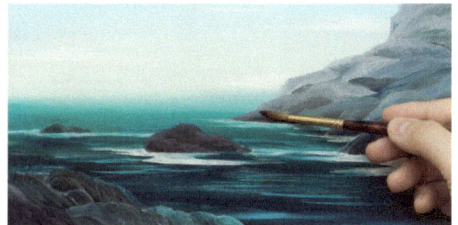

# Liquid Guache First Layer

The used transparent layer with very liquid gouache.

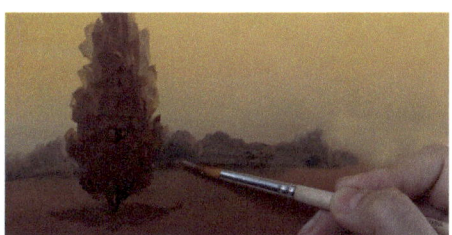

# Wash with Paint

Mix paints on to canvas without palette.

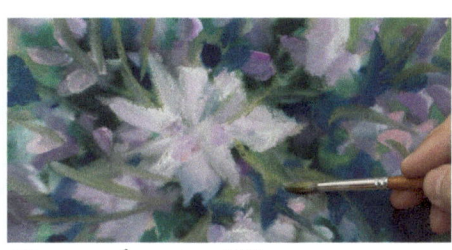

# Gouache-to-Wet

This is technique for applying brushstrokes on wet background.

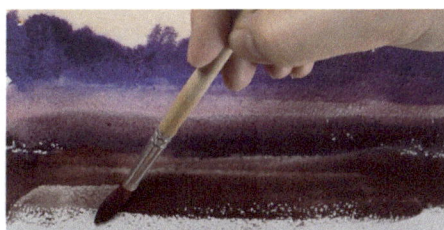

# Wash with Water

The use blending to dry paint of upper and low layers.

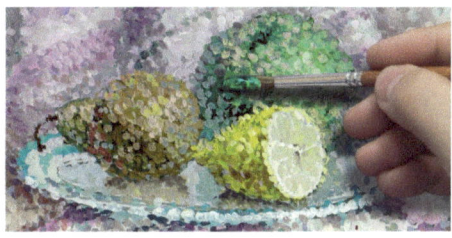

# Sharp and Multicolor Brushstrokes

Brushstrokes how mosaic. Every brushstroke separately, don't mixed with others.

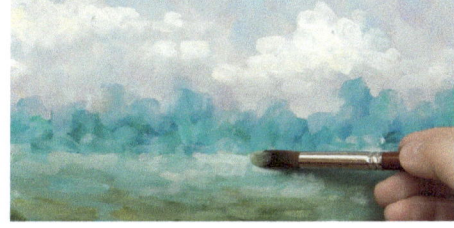

# Blurred Brushstrokes

The blurred brushstrokes are applied on dry background.

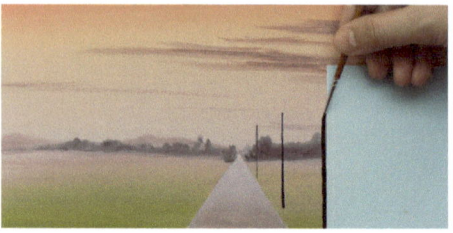

## Stencils and Masks

Stencil and mask used for corrected picture and adding elements.

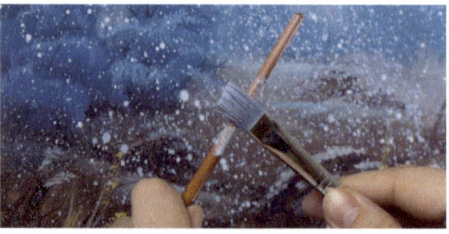

## Spattering

This can making a lot of small specks at picture.

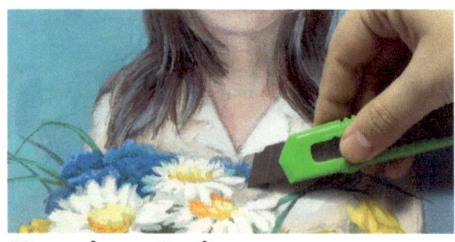

## Erasing Paint

If correction with other techniques can not used, then paint is erased.

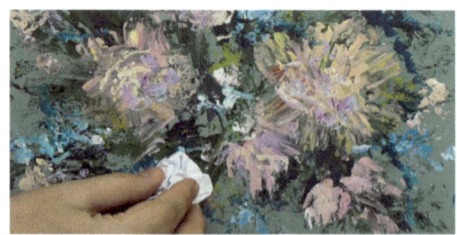

## Stamping

This technique is used for fill a area with same prints. Stamp can used as brush.

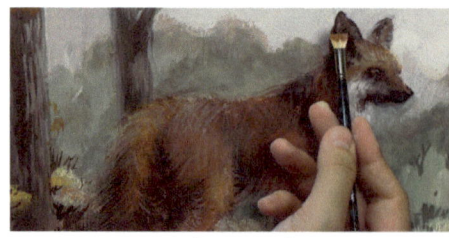

## Dray Brushwork

The dry brushwork used for create much thin stripes painted in the same direction.

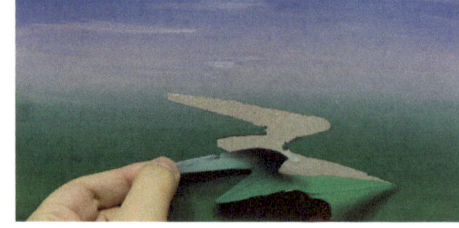

## Masking Support

The masking is used to isolate area of support from paint.